CW01664994

An Introduction to Digital Healthcare in the NHS. Edition Two.

Gary McAllister.
GaryECMcAllister@gmail.com
@garymcallister

For Laura…

Table of Contents

Preface

This short book is for professionals working within Healthcare IT, particularly in the NHS. As an introduction, this book is well suited to those who are considering changing careers and working in the Healthcare IT sector. The book aims to provide the reader with a summary of Healthcare IT in the NHS, covering patient flows, healthcare IT systems and modules, healthcare governance, some politics and finally a view of the future. I hope you enjoy reading this, please let me know what you think by contacting me at @garymcallister on Twitter.

Writing this book has taken a fair amount of effort and as with all literature requires support and commitment from peers and partners, ensuring the finished product is worthy of the consumption of the reader. This book is of no exception and I would like to thank the following people for the time taken to review and provide valuable feedback on this book.

Colin Sweeney (Ex Chief Information Officer at King's College Hospital) – thank you for your review as well as your humorous comments. They've made the process of correcting this work enjoyable.

Kate Dawes (Ex Strategy Director at Bromley Clinical Commissioning Group) – your comments and feedback were amazing, adding structure and rigour to this piece of work.

Michael Blount (PR Director) – your 3rd eye ensured that the content is consumable to a non-NHS person. I am sincerely grateful for your contribution.

Twitter community – all of the colleagues and friends who have supported the continued development of this book over social media. Thank you.

Mum and Dad – You are both solid as a rock and you've been on one hell of a journey. You've made it through together and your strength inspires me every single day. Thank you for taking the time to read this for me.

And finally, I'd like to thank my wonderful wife and my glorious children, who are simply my world. No matter what happens in my life and the pressures I am under, I always know there is love, smiles and happiness waiting for me at home.

At the time of writing (late 2020), we are on the verge of a vaccination for the COVID-19 virus, this has been a difficult time for all of us. If this has led to you transitioning to healthcare IT, firstly welcome, and secondly good luck on your journey.

Gary McAllister.

Introduction

Healthcare IT can be daunting, consisting of a series of acronyms and (sub)systems that can leave an individual confused. The journey (or pathway) of a patient with many illnesses (or co-morbidities) is complex and is likely to cross many care organisations. It is therefore important for someone with an interest in Healthcare IT to understand the differences between these interactions, who is responsible for treatment at each juncture and what IT systems and digital communications are likely to be exchanged in each care setting. This short introduction to Healthcare IT (in the NHS) explains the basics of what systems are used in each care setting and how these systems are integrated to minimise the duplication of information sent around the healthcare "system".

Before the advent of digital, healthcare was primarily a paper-driven industry. Patients would be assigned appointments using traditional diaries and letters would be typed using typewriters and sent to the patient. Patients would then be able to telephone the care provider to cancel and rebook their appointment. Once in hospital all activity captured during the patient stay would be recorded on paper and filed in folders called "the notes" and these would then be indexed using the patient's demographic details (name, date of birth, etc.). Once treated, the patient would be discharged with the relevant medication and the discharge information, or summary would be sent to the General Practitioner (GP) by post to manage the patient outside of the hospital. Fast forward to the 21st century and although a lot of the tasks in the process above are recorded digitally, all that has changed is that the paper is now replaced with an electronic equivalent but the fundamentals (and postage costs) remain the same[1].

This is all about to change though as the Healthcare landscape is becoming increasingly complex and more integrated, no longer is healthcare regarded as a differing series of isolated events between the General Practitioner (GP, Primary Care), the Acute Hospital (Secondary Care), Mental and Social Care. Health, Social and Mental healthcare are rightly becoming an integrated healthcare system. Having a full view of the patient's history and joining up the traditionally isolated disciplines enables complex patients to be managed more effectively, thus reducing the cost and the pressures on the healthcare system. The continued growth of Integrated Care Systems (ICSs) and their associated Digital Strategies are enforcing this modernised approach to healthcare. It is no longer acceptable for healthcare IT systems to be isolated, non-interoperable and have limited scalability.

Fast forward to the end of 2020, we are in wave two of the COVID-19 pandemic and healthcare has rapidly changed. The phrase "no one runs the IT department better than COVID-19" is no further from the truth. Due to social distancing and other restrictions (lockdowns etc.) care can no longer be provided in the traditional physical sense. This has led to an accelerated adoption of video and online services. I have dedicated a chapter to COVID-19 later in this book.

So, what is the difference between a Secondary Care Patient Administration System (PAS) and an Electronic Patient Record (EPR) system? How is information used for commissioning and population health? What are the differences between Primary, Secondary, Mental and Social Care IT? How do systems communicate in a healthcare environment? Why are clinical

---

[1] Caveat being GP summaries, these are generally sent digitally using either NHS Email or the Messaging Exchange for Social Care and Health (MESH), more on MESH later.

portals important in an interim period? What is the difference between radiology (imaging), pathology, microbiology and virology? What is the digital process of extracting a sample (blood, urine or faeces) and then getting the results of the requested diagnostic test electronically into the system? What is a ward-round, board-round, drug-round and observation-round and why are these important parts of a patient's stay in a hospital? How are hospitals paid? What is the Secondary Use Service, the Commissioning Dataset and what other submissions are important to primary and secondary care? This short introduction to Healthcare IT will provide the reader with a view on how these things are integrated and how Healthcare IT (in the NHS) is currently configured.

Chapter One - The NHS Healthcare System

The healthcare system in England consists of several layers and is governed by the Department of Health (DOH), the government department responsible for healthcare. Supporting the Department of Health is NHS England (Ireland, Scotland and Wales) who are responsible for the commissioning of Specialist Services[2] and GP services.

Although NHS[x] and NHS Digital are not strictly part of the payment and quality system, NHS[x] and Digital are having more of an influence on NHS contractual requirements. These are often published as Commissioning for Quality and Innovation (CQUINs) directives. An example of a CQUIN is the use of the Electronic Referral Service (ERS) which is discussed in more detail in Chapter Six – Entering the Healthcare System.

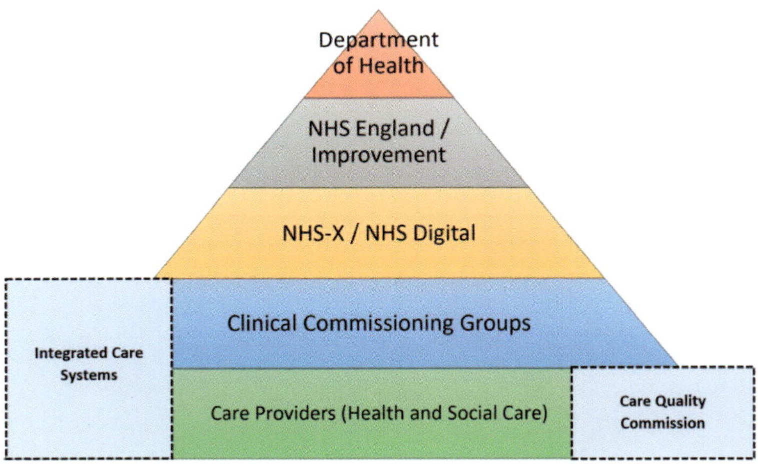

The Department of Health provides budgets to the Clinical Commissioning Groups (CCGs or ICSs – depending on the

[2] Services such as rare cancers, renal dialysis, and secure mental health services.

configuration). CCGs/ICSs are responsible for the contracting of healthcare services to the local population. There were originally 211 CCGs in England, but recently with the creation of Vanguard self-commissioning model(s) and continuing CCG mergers this number has reduced. CCGs are responsible for commissioning Urgent and Emergency Care, Out of Hours, Elective Hospital Care, Community, Rehabilitation, Maternity, Children's Services, Mental Health Services and Infertility Services.

CCGs are able to commission services on a 'block' or 'tariff' contract basis. Traditionally, services were all commissioned on a 'block' basis with funding provided to the care provider annually, regardless of the quality or quantity of care provided. The 'block' model pays the provider to deliver care, regardless of the throughput.

In England, this model has changed with 60% of secondary care services now commissioned on a tariff basis (although during COVID-19 all services were paid on block). A tariff payment model funds the care provider based on activity, with funding levels set based on nationally or locally agreed 'tariffs'. The payment-method and schedule is agreed between the CCG and the care providing organisation. Once agreed, the payment levels are then adjusted based on actual activity levels using the Secondary Use Services (SUS) and Commissioning Data Set (CDS) data submissions.

Each care providing organisation will have access to an informatics team that is responsible for the production of the SUS and the CDS data submissions. The correct production and population of these two files is arguably one of the most important aspects of the Healthcare IT landscape as these files are responsible for the payment of healthcare services.

For example, in the tariff model, the cost of an outpatient appointment is around £119 and the cost of a hip replacement is approximately £5,232. If an NHS Organisation were to carry out 10 outpatient appointments and 10 hip replacements they would be due a tariff payment of £53,510 on an agreed payment schedule. These activities will be captured in the SUS data file and reported to the commissioners for payment.

There is a fair amount of criticism of the CCG model with activity levels surpassing the budgets available to the CCGs (making CCGs an insolvent structure). This imbalance has led to unaffordable tariff changes, placing pressure on the healthcare system and placing many healthcare providers in financial deficit. These pressures led to the parliamentary-approved David Dalton review that promotes reconfiguration options for care providers to support the future sustainability of the healthcare system. For this reason it is likely healthcare services will progress back to block based payment models and regions will progress towards Integration Care System structures.

As the healthcare economy evolves Integrated Care Systems[3,4] or ICS will be established with the ability to commission, share services and provide appropriate care for the local population. This model has been progressed across England with 29 ICS being announced across the country (as at December 2020). A full list of these can be found on the NHS England website.

An Integrated Care System (ICS) spans both the commissioning and the providing organisations (including Local Authorities) to create a "care system". Care systems enable regions to have more control over how the budget is allocated and spent on health and care. Local control in this way allows regions to invest in areas which will have the most benefit for the population. This approach changes the dynamic of the previous CCG approach,

---

[3] https://www.kingsfund.org.uk/topics/integrated-care/accountable-care-organisations-explained

[4] https://www.england.nhs.uk/integratedcare/integrated-care-systems/

reducing the competition element of service provision with a more collaborative model of care delivery. A fundamental principle of the ICS delivery must be the delivery of value-based healthcare (the best value for the funding) rather than a pure focus on the cost of healthcare.

Financials aside, how are NHS Trusts governed and regulated from a quality, safety, efficiency and financial sustainability point of view? This is the responsibility of NHS Improvement and the Care Quality Commission (although NHS Improvement and NHS England have merged to form a yet to be titled commissioning and regulation organisation).

NHS Improvement is responsible for *working side-by-side* with Trusts to support the improvement of the quality of care as well as ensuring Trusts are operationally and financially viable. NHS Improvement carries out these duties by being a 'best practice hub', proposing changes in the management and delivery of patient care to assist making NHS Trusts more efficient.

In the event an NHS Trust is not performing to the required standard, NHS Improvement has a statutory right to step in and resolve issues so that NHS Trusts continue to meet the needs of the patient and budgetary constraints. As well as ensuring the performance of NHS organisations, NHS Improvement also regulates commissioning, ensuring that both procurement and tariffs are implemented legally and fairly.

As well as NHS Improvement, the Care Quality Commission regulate Health and Social Care Services in England. This includes all Hospitals, GPs, Dentists, Social Care and Community Services. The CQC operates by inspecting care organisations by using a panel of inspectors (including patients 'experts by experience') led by a lead CQC inspector. A CQC inspection is focused on the following criteria:

Safety – is the environment clean and are infection rates low?

Effectiveness – how good is the organisation at making people better, or improving quality of life?
Care – are the staff compassionate to patients and treat them as human beings?
Leadership – is the organisation well-led? Do staff have direction and a clear purpose?
Responsiveness – does the organisation listen and respond effectively to complaints?

Once an organisation has been inspected a 'CQC Report' is published for public information on the CQC website at http://www.cqc.org.uk/.

NHS^x

NHS^x was formed in 2019 to reform the adoption of Digital in Health and Social Care. NHS^x brings together the digital teams from the Department of Health, NHS England and NHS Improvement to create a national policy unit to reform digital in the health service.

The aim of NHS^x is to implement the Secretary of State's (Matthew Hancock at the time) technology vision[5] which is based on four principles:

- User need – improving the experience and adoption of IT solutions provided to the health and care service. Designing the solutions so that they are centred on user outcomes rather than just technology.

- Privacy and security – all solutions delivered into the health service must protect patient information, aligned to the Data Protection Act 2018 (GDPR) and promote trust with individuals.

---

5 http://bit.ly/hascitvision

- Interoperability and openness – data and information should flow between health services using open standards and open-source solutions.

- Inclusion – every solution should be accessible to individuals regardless of impairment needs.

As well as the above, NHS[x] is also responsible for the following service areas:

- Policy and strategy (including cyber) – defining and publishing technology policy and strategy.
- Transformation – is accountable for digital transformation and NHS Digital delivery.
- Standards – publication of national digitalisation standards.
- Delivery – delivery of user centred agile projects and other services (such as APIs) that improve digital adoption across the health and care service.
- Innovation – creation of incubation projects that may deliver innovation.
- Standardisation – promote standardisation (such as using the NHS App) for digital NHS interactions.
- Open – ensure that services and code is open for reuse across the NHS.
- Reforming procurement – change the approach and flexibility of procurement for digital services.
- Governance – review and promote effective governance for digital across the NHS.

More information on NHS[x] can be found on the website at https://www.nhsx.nhs.uk/.

Chapter Two – The Ten-Year (Long Term) Plan

In 2018 the government announced that the NHS will receive an additional £20.5billion pounds of funding for health services. This was announced alongside a refreshed ten year 'Long Term Plan' (published in January 2019) for the NHS to support the sustainability and transformation agenda.

Central to the plan and a common theme across the health and care sector is the need to enable patients to become more empowered and take ownership of their care. The long plan introduces new concepts such as remote monitoring, population health management and a change in how appointments are conducted (using voice and video consultations instead of face to face).

As well as the digital elements of the Long-Term Plan, the plan summary[6] is structured on the following areas:

- **Making sure everyone gets the best start in life** – improving the outcomes during and post pregnancy, supporting mental health for mothers and babies and reducing childhood obesity.

- **Delivering world-class care for major health problems** – reducing heart attacks, strokes and dementia, improving exercise for those with heart conditions, supporting those with mental health issues and diagnosing cancer earlier.

---

[6] https://www.longtermplan.nhs.uk/wp-content/uploads/2019/01/the-nhs-long-term-plan-summary.pdf

- **Supporting people to age well** – improving the funding available to primary and community care, investing in community 'rapid response teams', empowering patients to have more control over when and where they receive their care.

The NHS Long Term Plan outlines 'how' these outcomes will be achieved with additional funding and an implementation framework with guidance for the health system. This is supported by five delivery ambitions that are provided in the Long-Term Plan summary document:

- **Doing things differently** – Empower patients to have more control over their healthcare as well as implement 'Primary Care Networks' (PCN's) which will enable GP's and Community Services to collaborate together to improve health outcomes for local populations. As well as the introduction of Primary Care Networks the NHS will focus on value and collaboration-based healthcare services through the formation of Integration Care Systems.

- **Preventing illness and tacking health inequalities** – Reducing high risk health conditions that are common in deprived areas such as alcohol and tobacco addiction. The plan proposes a reduction in the prevalence of type-2 diabetes and support for communities to become healthier.

- **Backing our workforce** – The NHS will focus on staff wellbeing and training. The plan has a particular focus on adding additional nurses, GPs and care providers. Additional staffing programmes such as apprenticeships and funding the training of the required roles in the NHS is seen as key to the future success of the service.

- **Making better use of data and digital technology** – Improve the use and adoption of technology in the NHS. The plan progresses the development of the "NHS App" which has since been positioned as a portal to other services. Additional use of data is prevalent in the plan so that health and care is delivered based on population need rather than anecdotal/policy driven provision.

- **Getting the most out of taxpayers' investment in the NHS** – Ensure that the provision of healthcare is as efficient as possible, limiting the amount of waste that may exist across the health service.

Chapter Three – Identifying the Patient

Now that you've covered the NHS plan and governance structure it is time to cover some of the fundamentals of NHS-IT. Every hospital, GP, community or social care system will retain a unique identifier for the patient. These identifiers are used throughout the patients care, ensuring that there is a single reference point for the record.

There tends to be two identifiers for a patient in most care environments:

- **Local Identifier** – is often referred to as the hospital number in secondary care (hospital environments). These identifiers are assigned when the patient is first registered with the care providing organisation and are used as the identifier for the patient in all local systems and paper services ('the notes'). The local identifier ensures that tests, observations, prescriptions and diagnostics all correlate to the correct patient.

  IT systems that can produce a local identifier in secondary care are usually the Emergency Department (A&E) system, the maternity system or the patient administration system (PAS). It is common for this process to be managed as a pre-allocated range of numbers against a master index and although other systems can generate hospital numbers it is usually the PAS system that is the single source of truth for patient numbering. More on the PAS system later.

- **NHS Number** – are assigned by the national Personal Demographic Service (PDS) which was commissioned as part of the National Programme for IT (NPfIT) Spine IT Services. The NHS Number is the national identifier for the patient and is assigned when a patient first registers with the NHS (usually at birth). NHS Numbers are provided electronically by the Personal Demographic Service (PDS) through a 'tracing service' and are integrated with Maternity systems (at birth), GP systems and hospital demographic systems. Tracing can be achieved in real-time (at registration) or via a batch process. The tracing service attempts to match the patient based on the provided demographics and if successful will return the NHS Number, if the tracing is unsuccessful a new NHS Number will be provided by the tracing service.

The NHS Number is an exciting concept and one that is being used across care economies to 'join-up' care. An example of this is the Local Care Record[7] in South East London which uses the NHS Number as the sole identifier to join up records from over 140 care providing organisations in the boroughs of Southwark, Lambeth and Bromley.

Although there is a national ambition for the NHS Number to become the sole identifier for a patient across the NHS, this is a difficult target to achieve as some patients have not originated from the NHS (such as foreign visitors) and due to legacy constraints almost all hospitals use the local hospital number to identify the paper notes.

A full explanation as to the technical details and how these identifiers are used can be found in Chapter Twelve – Interoperability Primer.

[7] http://www.kingshealthpartners.org/localcarerecord

Chapter Four – Digital Healthcare Modules

A modern digital healthcare system is managed by several major IT systems (or modules). A care organisation will tend to have one of two strategies, a 'best-of-breed' strategy or a 'Big Electronic Health Record (EHR)' strategy. Neither of these strategies are right or wrong, both have pros and cons. The debate tends to conclude that a Big EHR limits flexibility but enforces consistency and safety, whereas a best-of-breed strategy promotes flexibility and innovation but restricts consistency and safety.

A best-of-breed care organisation will traditionally purchase many IT systems and integrate them together using a communication standard such as Health Level 7 (HL7) which is explained in detail in Chapter Twelve – Interoperability Primer – whereas a Big EHR organisation will tend to try and solve the majority of the challenges using a 'big' core solution that comprises of several tightly coupled modules.

In the United States the trend is moving towards the Big EHR approach due to the $30billion funding injection and the associated requirements of the Health Insurance and Portability and Accountability Act (HIPAA[8]). A Big EHR simplifies statutory reporting as well as enhances productivity and safety through the use of a single solution. Although it is important to note that a Big EHR will not deliver all of the specialist functionality needed in most large teaching hospitals.

Below is a summary of the core modules of an Electronic Health Record used in a hospital setting as well as their role in a healthcare organisation.

8

https://en.wikipedia.org/wiki/Health_Insurance_Portability_and_Accountability_Act

Mental Health organisations tend to use a subset of these modules and have a reliance on rich documentation functionality. Although the documentation requirements of Mental Health are more extensive, the expectations and principles regarding digitalisation are the same. Primary care is equally similar in the need to hold a set of patient records, store notes, book appointments etc.

These can be delivered either modularly (Big EHR) or singularly (Best of Breed).

Management and Efficiency Modules

- **Patient Administration System (PAS) Module** – is responsible for the registration of the patient with the care providing organisation, the receipt of referrals, scheduling of appointments (outpatients, scheduling, booking) and the management of the hospital bed allocation (inpatients). A key component of the PAS is to deliver waiting list functionality so that patients are seen within the appropriate 'referral to treatment (RTT)' target (which is currently 18 weeks). PAS modules often provide the functionality to print and send appointment letters to patients and in more advanced systems may provide functionality for text-messaging/app based reminders/notifications.

- **Bed Management Module** – often an integrated module of the PAS, the Bed Management Module provides visibility of beds in the care environment. Beds often go through many 'states' before being made available for a patient (such as requiring cleaning or changing) and beds are often 'tagged' for use for specific purposes (such as sexual orientation, infection control, isolated patients, or cardiac monitored patients).

Effective bed management supports nurses and doctors with appropriate discharge planning and enables hospitals to manage occupancy more efficiently.

- **Staffing Module**[9] – in order to deliver safe care, it is important that the correct levels of staffing are provided. Staffing levels are determined based on the 'wellness' of a patient. For example, a patient in intensive care is likely to have a 1:1 staffing ratio, whereas patients on an elderly care ward may have a differing ratio. It is down to the organisation to determine what safe staffing levels are for their patient needs. This information is often captured electronically using formulas such as the safer nursing tool kit.

- **Single Sign On** – is a piece of software that runs on the clinical computer and uses biometric (fingerprints, iris scanner, facial recognition) or smart-card (such as a contactless bank card) technology to log the clinical user into the existing IT clinical systems.

  Although not strictly part of an Electronic Health Record system, Single Sign On is an unavoidable technology required in complex healthcare environments. Single Sign On reduces the burden of clinical staff needing to remember multiple usernames and passwords. This is achieved by the software remembering the passwords used by the user and inputting these passwords automatically into the clinical systems when they are launched. This reduces the need for clinical staff to have to type passwords into multiple IT systems, allowing more time for clinical staff to treat the patient.

---

[9] https://www.england.nhs.uk/ourwork/safe-staffing/

- **Theatres Module** – provides the ability to schedule the operating theatre at specific times for specific operations, capture pre-and post-operation digital notes and ensure that all of the theatre equipment is scheduled and booked in and out of theatre for safety reasons. The theatres module includes activity monitoring and reporting to ensure that theatres are utilised to the most effective capacity.

- **Emergency Department Module** – An Emergency Department (ED) system is used to register the patient and ensure that the patient conforms to the national emergency department waiting times (4-hours). It is common for ED systems to allow the requesting of diagnostic tests, enable patients to be allocated to different zones (such as Major Injuries, Minor Injuries and Resuscitation for seriously wounded patients). ED is covered in more detail in Chapter Eleven – Out of Hours, Emergency, 111 and London Ambulance.

Clinical Modules

- **Order Communication Module** – is a vital component of the digital healthcare system. An order is a complex construct, made of one or many 'order items' but is mostly used for diagnostic test requesting. Think of an order the same as buying a book online. You go to Amazon, place an order for your item(s) and then an individual (or robot) in the warehouse will fulfil your order and send you the item(s) in response.

  When a clinical member of staff decides to place an order, a digital form is completed in the order communications module and this order is then sent to the order fulfilling department. In the case of a laboratory test, an order is placed in the order communications module and this order is then sent to the laboratory for testing. At the time of requesting the order a barcoded label is also printed and attached to the blood sample (which should be taken from the patient at the time the order is placed). This printed label includes the identifier of the order which is sent to the laboratory module along with the required test details. Once the order is placed, the sample is sent to the laboratory and the required diagnostics are performed. The results from the diagnostics are then sent electronically to the results module for review by the requesting clinician or a member of their team.

It is important to note that the laboratory or receiving department can challenge an order request. This may result in the receiving department (laboratory) cancelling the order and replacing the request with a more appropriate (or cheaper) alternative.

- **Results (Acknowledgement) Module** – provides an overview of the results of ordered diagnostic tests. This module is usually dynamic and has the ability to show information in a tabular format, using graphs, a written format and even display media by linking to an image or a document in an associated system. As well as displaying the result it is common for modern Electronic Health Record systems to also contain a results acknowledgement component that audits the review of results within specified timescales.

- **Observations Module** – observations are an integral component of an Electronic Health Record system and enable the capture of vital signs such as heart-rate, temperature and oxygen levels. Observations are used to monitor patients during their stay in hospital and are typically captured every 1 to 4 hours. Often completed by nursing staff, observations support early warning scores that identify the sickest patients in a hospital.

- **Maternity Module** – is responsible for the management and care of both the mother and the foetus/baby through the pre-natal and post-natal stages of birth. The maternity module includes specialist charting and reporting. Once the baby is born it is common for the maternity system to officially register the baby with the NHS Personal Demographics Service (PDS). The NHS Number is then used to identify the baby for the rest of their life.

- **Child Health Module** – provide specialist algorithms and forms related to children's health. For example, the child health module often includes vaccination records, growth charts and paediatric observation charts with knowledge of the differing variables required to safely care for children.

- **Community and Out of Hospital Module** – is provided for care workers who need to visit patients outside of the hospital environment (in their home). This module provides out of hospital scheduling, offline access to patient records and enables community care workers to record information about their patient from their homes. Community care is an important strategic aspect of the care system and as the ageing population grows it is likely more care will be delivered out of hospital.

- **Radiology/Imaging Module** – integrates with the Picture Archiving and Communication System (PACS) and Vendor Neutral Archive system. The Radiology Module provides the Examination Identifier for an imaging study and supports the scheduling of the people, equipment and patient for the imaging service. A radiology module provides the ability for radiologists to review the images and report or 'result' the images to the Results Module.

- **Pathology, Microbiology and Virology (Labs) Module** – provides the ability for laboratory staff to manage the flow of samples through the laboratory workflow. Modern laboratories are comparable to conveyer belts where samples are booked in and then managed through the laboratory. A typical journey for a laboratory sample is as follows;

    - Booked in / received – the sample is received in the laboratory and the appropriate test is scheduled using the barcode sticker on the sample. The sticker ensures that correct patient information is included and diagnostics are performed on the sample.

    - Analysing / in-progress – the sample is being analysed.

    - Performed – the analysis is completed and the results are available for laboratory staff to review.

    - Results available / results reviewed / reported – the results are reported against the sample and are either sent electronically to the results module (as an interim result) or are reviewed and finalised by the lab technician and sent to the results module for clinical review.

- **Infection Management Module** – enables the configuration and management of infection control in the hospital environment. It is important for hospitals to identify and limit the spread of infection using infection screening and isolation methods at the point of admission and during a hospital stay.

Electronic systems assist with this by allowing infection control specialists the ability to configure the associated parameters against a patient sample that triggers specific infections. For example, the Methicillin-Resistant Staphylococcus Aureus (MRSA) bacteria is identified by taking swabs on admission, these swabs are tested for identification of antibiotic resistance and the results are processed electronically and the associated infection alert will then be raised if MRSA is identified.

- **Prescribing and Drug (Stock) Management Module** – Electronic Prescribing and Medicines Administration (EPMA) contributes to enhanced safety in a hospital. The digital prescribing and scheduling of prescriptions ensures that drugs are administered within the correct timeframe and safely administered on the correct schedules. Electronic prescribing supports stock management by enabling hospitals to replenish drug stock more effectively rather than continuing to over or under order medicines.

  Modern Electronic Health Records enforce the electronic identification of the patient before the drug is dispensed from secure (bedside) cabinets, only allowing the release of the appropriate drug once the patient has been correctly identified.

- **Documentation Module** – clinical documentation is captured throughout the patient's care and a generic documentation module supports the specialist capture of documentation. A documentation 'set' is usually created to support specialist and generic data capture at the point of care. Documentation consists of mandatory information such as symptoms, presenting complaints and diagnosis to speciality-specific information such as oncology/cancer staging data. Clinical documentation is presented as a series of forms along with specialist tools such as drawing, diagnosis or procedure capture used to enforce 'coding' of clinical information.

As well as clinical documentation, the documentation module should provide the functionality to allow correspondence with the patient and other care providers. These outputs are created in the form of reports or other electronic communications and are shared using electronic communication (Email, CDA) or a printing module.

- **Specialist Modules** – as well as the core modules mentioned above, each vendor may venture into specialist areas of the anatomy or clinical service such as genomics, cardiac, respiratory, renal, ophthalmology or a cancer module. The options for specialisation are broad and would need to be considered on a per EHR basis.

  In general, Big EHR vendors struggle to provide comprehensive specialist modules so ensure your requirements are clear and that your due diligence process is robust before committing to specialist EHR modules.

Shared Modules

As well as the above modules, a good EHR platform will enable the following cross-module functionality.

- **Positive Patient Identification** – positive patient identification enforces the identification of a patient at the point of care (usually at the bedside) before carrying out a healthcare related activity. This is achieved using either biometrics (such as finger print scanning or face recognition) or scanning a barcoded wrist band. Once identified, the EHR system will then allow the user to carry out the activity requested prior to identification (such as taking blood or administering medicines).

- **Scheduling Module** – scheduling is fundamental to good patient care. Inadequate scheduling leads to wasted patient visits and potentially missing equipment. A good scheduling module will enable the coordination of a patient visit and the appropriate staff, equipment, rooms and follow-up at the right time, in the correct order. Good scheduling is a complex exercise but can be drastically simplified with an EHR system with the appropriate scheduling rules.

- **Check-in and Digital Signage Module** – a check-in and signage module reduces the need for reception staff at patient treatment locations. When the patient is sent their letter or appointment notification the correspondence will include a barcode or radio frequency identifier (RFID) chip. The patient is then able to use this letter to 'check-in' to their appointment when they arrive at the destination. Digital Signage (TV screens) are then used to prompt the patient to go to the appropriate consulting room from the waiting area.

- **Task Management Module** – provides the ability to create tasks both automatically and manually. Automatic tasks are generated following an event in the system, whereas manual tasks are created by a user of the system. Tasks can be assigned to groups or teams of clinical staff and are important for ensuring activities such as portering (moving a patient around), administering medication, reviewing results and documenting a patient visit are all completed within a given period. These periods are usually monitored for safety reasons so that patient activity is managed appropriately.

- **Rules Engine (Medical Logic Modules, MLMs)** – logic rules enable users of the system to add functionality to the system. For example, if a series of safety checks are required when a medication order is placed (such as ensuring that drugs do not interact, potentially causing harm), a logic engine can carry out these rules and enable new rules to be added to the system without requesting a change from the software vendor. Rules also enable activities to be created and managed within the system, such as tasks, scheduled events or orders.

- **Alerting** – Alerts are used to enforce clinical safety and to inform clinical and non-clinical staff about events or activities. An alert can be electronic (sent to mobile devices or via email) or they can be presented on-screen (as a result from a Logic Module or an erroneous user action).

  Alerts are important to remind users to follow the safety rules of the system and they prevent possible harm to the patient. An example of an alert would be raising an on-screen prompt to remind the user that an MRSA screen is completed at admission or warning the user that the prescribing of a particular medication will cause potential adverse interactions with an existing medication/or interact with a patients allergy.

- **Specialised Views (Portals)** – portals are often included as part of an EHR system to enable other clinical IT systems to present information into the core

EHR. Portals are considered generation one or generation two.

- A generation one portal will present information using views from an existing system. The information is presented 'as is' and is incorporated using integrated windows.

- A generation two portal can connect directly to the data in the existing clinical systems and seamlessly integrate the information with the primary EHR. Generation two portals also tend to provide the same functionality as a generation one portal. This approach ensures that information can be accessed regardless of the technical capabilities supported by existing systems. A major limitation of portals is that the targeted system needs to be 'open' for access to the information, which is often not the case with healthcare IT systems.

Portals are generally web/internet based, meaning they can only be accessed using an internet web browser (such as Microsoft's Internet Explorer/Google Chrome). In the case of older IT systems, the approach for access is usually managed using a Single Sign-On context management engine. A Single Sign-On context management engine allows the portal to log in to the older IT system, select the appropriate patient and present the relevant clinical details. This is all managed by a piece of software that is run on the clinical user's computer and the 'clicks' are automated by the software to present the appropriate patient's details.

Portals do not tend to allow information to be shared between the EHR and the targeted systems. The best way to cover interoperability is to ensure that your clinical IT systems support good standards such as Health Level 7 (FHIR). HL7 is covered in more detail in Chapter Twelve – Interoperability Primer.

- **Electronic Communication** – IT systems must be able to communicate with other IT systems, system users or in the case of an EHR the patient (using an app or patient accessible website). In a healthcare setting this is generally achieved by the use of email or interoperable system messaging (where the system talks to another system to provide information on what is happening). Healthcare traditionally relies on a legacy technology called HL7 to allow systems to communicate with each other. HL7 is covered in detail in Chapter Twelve – Interoperability Primer. As well as HL7 it is common for EHR systems to support several other methods of communication such as email, instant messaging, mobile phone text messaging and more recently app-based push notifications. All of these communication methods can be triggered using the Rules or Logic modules provided by most EHR systems.

- **Speech and Voice Recognition** – the use of keyboards and mice is a rate limiting factor in the productive use of an EHR. The leading EHR solutions therefore have integrated voice recognition technology (Nuance or 3M M*Model as an example). Voice recognition enables the clinical users to control the software using their voice, which then transcribes the information directly into the medical record. This improves productivity by reducing the need to type all correspondence using the keyboard.

- **Mobility and Remote Access** – with the introduction of the Apple iPad and iPhone there is an expectation that computer systems will be available from tablet devices and mobile phones. The creation of mobile apps requires additional engineering by the EHR vendor and it is common for the app to provide limited functionality to the desktop (PC) version. Apps can also be used and accessed outside of a hospital boundary and this should be expected from any EHR app implementation. External access requires additional security and information governance controls to be in place, more on this in Chapter Fourteen – Information Governance (IG) and SecurityChapter Fourteen – Information Governance (IG) and Security.

- **Patient Access** – Patient Held Records (PHRs) shift the responsibility of the management of data away from the care provider and into the hands of the patient. Enabling patient access to their medical record provides an opportunity for healthcare providers to empower the patient to book their own appointments, review results and communicate with healthcare professionals online. This approach also improves patient attendance and reduces the administration overheads on the healthcare provider. Patient Access provides the opportunity for Patient Recorded Outcome Measures (PROMS), a principle that means patient treatment should not just be measured based on the care provider's perspective of success but also the continued wellbeing of the patient.

- **Collaboration Technology and Video Integration** – Using digital collaboration enables clinicians and patients to access care services without the need to travel to the care provider. The integration of video and collaboration services enables clinicians and patients to communicate with each other without needing to use traditional telephone or face to face consultation methods. These remote access modules will fundamentally change how healthcare services are delivered.

Following the COVID-19 pandemic these modules and other specialist systems have now become a mainstream component of the healthcare delivery model. Due to COVID-19 visitation, outpatient attendance/appointments, therapy sessions and other non-critical services have moved to virtual service models.

- **Patient and Equipment Tracking** – some EHR solutions come with a patient and equipment tracking module which allows digital tracking in the care environment. Tracking is a good solution for infection management as well as looking after frail and elderly patients who may not have the cognitive abilities to find their way around a hospital, or who may get themselves lost whilst staying in hospital. Equipment tracking in large complex organisations reduces the loss of equipment and ensures that equipment is in the right place at the right time.

Estates Management Modules

- **Portering and patient transport** – these modules provide the ability to request a porter (who are the individuals who move patients around the hospital / between appointments or diagnostic services) and to request external transport services. There is often a limited number of porters in a hospital and therefore a task based portering solution is important for requesting a portering 'job'.

  Patient transport services track and manage the scheduling of transport for patients/equipment that needs to move outside a hospital or between hospital sites. These modules may integrate with taxi companies or private ambulance services.

- **Meal ordering / Catering** – the catering system often integrates with bedside devices or ward-based tablets to allow patients to order their meal choices. The modules also help with stock ordering and the reduction of food waste.

Analytics and Coding Modules

Analytics and coding modules enable the use of data within the EHR to support performance management, episode costing, healthcare analytics and research.

- **Clinical Coding Module** – supports the national data sets by enabling coding staff to 'code' the patient record. Coding is important for costing of a patient's stay in hospital and this is usually associated with the diagnosis or procedures performed whilst the patient was in hospital. Coding is often captured using a 3rd party module and then fed into the PAS Module for billing purposes (3M Medicode is the most prevalent system for this purpose).

- **Informatics/Analytics Module** – is required to provide intelligence on the activities carried out within the care environment. It is common for the informatics module to enable the creation of dashboards, scorecards and ad-hoc reports. The informatics module is responsible for the creation and validation of national and regional submissions for services such as the Secondary Use Service and supporting the Commissioning Data Set. These are vital data submissions that must be correct and may have an impact on income if they are not. A complete list of data sets can be found on the NHS Digital website at http://www.content.digital.nhs.uk/datasets.

- **Population Health Management** – as the healthcare system evolves it is becoming more important to measure healthcare on a population basis. Measuring healthcare outcomes on a population basis will help identify any variations in the management of care across healthcare institutions or care economies. This is common practice in the United States as single healthcare institutions cover the population of several million people.

Although a Big EHR often delivers the core elements required to run a care environment, it is still common for large specialist care organisations to need specialist IT systems.

Each organisation should consider whether the effort of configuring and maintaining a Big EHR outweighs the benefits of procuring a specialist system. Specialist 'proprietary' systems are often configured to meet national or specialist data submission guidelines which take a considerable effort to replicate into an EHR.

Chapter Five – NHS Procurement

This chapter will provide the appropriate guidance for procuring an EHR or similar digital solution in the health service.

Procurement is the process of finding and agreeing terms (a contract) for goods or works from a third party. Procurement is especially important in a public organisation as expenditure needs to be transparent and deliver value for money. It is therefore important that all procurement complies with the EU Public Contracts Directive[10] and the UK Statutory Instrument 2015 regulations (inclusive of the EU Exit amendments)[11].

Procurement in the NHS should be conducted using a bidding or tendering process. This is where requirements are documented and suppliers respond to the tender with their ability to meet the required specification. Alternatively, a request for goods is placed on to the open market with the best price/value being awarded for the requested materials.

Once created, the detailed tender specification is placed onto a marketplace for suppliers to respond. Following the supplier response, the tendering organisation should conduct a scoring/evaluation/dialogue exercise on each submission to award the tender to the preferred supplier.

This is the simplest form of tendering exercise, but with larger procurements it is common for a Pre-qualification/Invitation to Participate in Dialogue (IPD) shortlisting and a competitive dialogue process to be conducted. This ensures that the proposed financial and contractual terms meet the specified requirements, that the supplier meets any specialist needs of the

---

[10] https://eur-lex.europa.eu/legal-content/EN/TXT/?uri=celex%3A32019R1828

[11] https://www.legislation.gov.uk/ukdsi/2020/9780348212952

project, and that a competitive process is used to obtain best value for money.

Sometimes the tender process is unnecessary, especially when there is only a single supplier in the market for a given requirement (such as End of Life Microsoft software maintenance). When that is the case, a single tender purchase should be allowed by exception.

There are generally three ways to procure services in the NHS.

1. Official Journal of the European Union (OJEU) / Find a tender (FTS) – OJEU is the official gazette of record for the European Union and is published daily. The journal comprises of two formal series (L and C) which are used for regulation, with competition announcements published on the S series - the series used for publishing procurement opportunities.

   Following the United Kingdom exit from the European union new procurement guidance has been issued[12]. This guidance suggests the use of a new gazette known as the Find a Tender service (FTS). Find a tender will replace the UKs use of OJEU for the tender of goods/services on the 31st December 2020.

2. Procurement Framework – a procurement framework is an OJEU/Find a Tender compliant pre-qualified framework for goods or services. Frameworks reduce the time for procurement as standard contract terms are already agreed and suppliers are added based on a proven ability to meet functional, non-functional, legal and legislative requirements of the framework.

---

[12] https://www.gov.uk/guidance/public-sector-procurement-from-1-january-2021

3. G-Cloud – is a procurement framework and digital marketplace for cloud-based commodity technology. G-Cloud has a lower barrier of entry, thus enabling smaller-to-medium-size businesses to register and conduct business in the public sector.

All of this may seem excessive to purchase something that may not hold much value. For this reason, there are often Standing Financial Instructions (SFIs) documented in each organisation which set the thresholds on how purchasing exercises should take place. For example:

- The goods/services have a value less than £10,000 – the item can often be directly purchased from a supplier as long as the cost is deemed best value for the organisation and that the total purchase from the supplier will not breach other thresholds.

- Over £10,000 but less than £122,976 – three quotes for the purchase should be obtained from the supply chain and the cheapest quote (unless by exception) must be used to purchase the goods.

- Equal to or greater than £122,976 – a full EU/FTS compliant procurement exercise must be conducted to purchase the goods or services. This is the required process for goods or services of this value by law. For clarity, procurement frameworks are almost always OJEU/FTS compliant.

Spending limits change annually and these may change again following Brexit. I'd recommend visiting https://www.gov.uk/government/publications/procurement-policy-note-new-thresholds-2020 for the most up to date procurement regulations.

Below is a list of pointers you may wish to consider when conducting large procurements. Please ensure you contact your local procurement and/or legal expert prior to attempting to conduct any procurement exercise. If you are unsure always get professional advice prior to any purchasing decisions.

1. **Limit your up-front exposure** – no matter what you are purchasing, always limit your up-front exposure. All purchasing should be aligned to planned milestones and deliverables.

   Ensure there is risk funding in the project for any fluctuations in pricing (such as exchange rates) or likely commercial or scope variation during the project.

2. **Always have clear exit and break clauses** – ensure that both exit and break clauses are in the contract and cover responsibilities, timescales and expectations. Ensure that the projects are structured so that you can exit the relationship whenever convenient for both parties.

3. **Purchase services, not technology** – although tempting, try not to purchase a product or specific technology. Conduct your procurements with a vendor neutral attitude with clear objectives (user-centric) and measurable requirements. This will drive competition in the procurement process.

4. **Sign off a detailed plan as part of the contract** – a realistic plan and series of milestones should be agreed between the parties prior to contract signature. Once completed, the plan should be used as a measure for contract variance, ensuring that both parties understand their responsibilities and accountability for delivery.

5. **Ensure that there are rewards and penalties in the contract** – the contract is a two-way agreement with the supply chain. Reward the supplier for early delivery and equally have penalties in the contract for late or non-delivery (these are known as liquidated damages).

6. **Insist on benchmarking clauses in the contract** – if you are procuring a service, insist on independent benchmarking in the contract so that you can be assured that you are always receiving value for money.

7. **Agree gain-sharing and reduction incentives** – the value of goods often reduces in the technology marketplace and therefore the cost of service should also reduce. If possible, agree an equal saving scheme with the supplier so that they are incentivised to reduce the cost of service over the life of the agreement.

8. **Make sure upgrades and continual service improvement is covered** – do not purchase long-life point-in-time services. Make sure that upgrades, patching and maintenance is covered in the service schedule of the contract. Ensure that a service improvement plan is factored into at least a quarterly service review schedule.

9. **Invest in robust legal, commercial and procurement advice throughout the procurement and beyond** – no matter how good you think you are at procurement, contract negotiation and management you will never be as good as a trained professional in this area.

10. **Agree organisationally aligned service level agreements** – make sure the support hours and response times are aligned to the business hours, no one wants an Accident and Emergency Department offline over a weekend whilst the supplier's staff have left the office. Ensure that service response and break/fix times

are covered, also include performance, maintenance, backup/recovery and monitoring service levels in the contract.

11. **The stakeholders and users are responsible for the specification** – any procurement should be led by the stakeholder and user community. IT should be considered the enabler for the outcomes and functions specified by the stakeholder and user group.

12. **Add contingency for requirement changes post procurement** – It is common for requirements to change during and following the procurement exercise, this needs to be catered for from a budget and contracting perspective.

Now that you've specified and purchased your EHR with a robust contract, let's learn how the healthcare system works in the NHS.

Chapter Six – Entering the Healthcare System

Entering the healthcare system is possible in a number of ways. This chapter explains the most common first point of contact with the NHS, the General Practitioner (GP).

Usually a patient will enter the healthcare system following a visit to their GP and this visit may result in a secondary care referral[13] (a request for treatment/review at a hospital), a GP may also request a referral to services such as Mental Health (counselling) or other therapies such as Physio. A patient may also enter the healthcare system as the result of a visit to the Emergency Department (A&E). In some cases, patients will enter the healthcare system following a social care referral or a mental health referral/admission.

At times patients are referred from one hospital to another for specialist treatment and this is known as a specialist/tertiary referral. A common example of this is for specialist cancer (oncology) treatment.

Each of these scenarios will have an associated digital impact, these are covered below.

GP Referrals to hospital

Typically patients enter the healthcare system via their GP (Primary Care). A patient will present to their GP with a set of symptoms, the GP will triage the symptoms and if appropriate attempt an initial phase one treatment. If the initial treatment is unsuccessful the GP will refer the patient to the appropriate

---

[13] A referral is the redirecting of a patient to a specialist or appropriate practitioner.

practitioner in a specialist (hospital) setting[14] - hospitals are otherwise known as secondary care. A GP referral can be carried out manually (by writing to a specialist) or electronically using the national NHS Digital supplied Electronic Referral Service (ERS, previously Choose and Book). In 2017, NHS England published a Commissioning for Quality and Innovation (CQUIN)[15] incentive to encourage the use of ERS as from the 1st October 2018. From this date, Trusts will not be paid for any referrals received outside of the ERS system. Effectively ERS is the source of truth for requests for care from hospitals, resulting in an outpatient appointment. GPs will get an extra £1 for every referral placed using the Electronic Referral Service.

> CQUINs are an important aspect of the continuous improvement of healthcare. CQUINS often become contractually binding over a period of time and are becoming more dependent on technology. For example, the 2015/16 CQUIN for Acute Kidney Injury (AKI) required an AKI staging score[16] based on a nationally agreed algorithm, which analyses patient blood results to produce the score. Staging patients manually would require a significant amount of resource so organisations rightly decided to implement the AKI algorithm electronically based on the analysis of existing blood results.

During the GP consultation, the GP will make a decision that the patient requires a specialist referral. The GP then accesses the national ERS using their GP Information System (EMIS, Vision, TPP or Microtest) through an integrated 'button' in the

---

[14] Or alternative specialist/therapy provider, it is also possible for hospital to hospital referrals.

[15] http://content.digital.nhs.uk/media/23488/NHS-e-Referral-Service-CQUIN-Guidance/pdf/e-RS_CQUIN_Supplementary_Guidance_Feb_17_Final.pdf

[16] https://www.england.nhs.uk/wp-content/uploads/2014/06/psa-aki-alg.pdf

system. Once within ERS the GP can then search for the required specialist, select the appropriate appointment slot and book the patient's referral appointment.

ERS is a challenge for consuming organisations as the referral system does not allow visibility of the referral prior to booking the appointment (although this is possible by using the ERS technology it is still not integrated in most hospitals) and requires Trusts to publish all appointment slots on the ERS system. ERS does not take into account telephone or digital clinics, walk-ins, follow-ups or other appointment types. A criticism of ERS is that it is a 'one-way' system; the service takes the GP's decision as final and does not allow the Secondary Care provider to review, discuss or 'vet' the referral prior to the appointment being allocated.

NHS Digital have created a series of Application Programmable Interfaces (APIs)[17] that enable Secondary Care organisations to interact more effectively with the service. It provides Trusts earlier visibility of the referral, allowing organisations to ensure patients are receiving the correct care. The ERS roadmap also has the intention to introduce advanced electronic triage of the referral before allowing GPs to book hospital appointments. Due to COVID-19 and the accelerated shift to digital, almost all non-urgent referrals are being managed digitally using telehealth.

Although ERS provides the scope for the initial appointment, the system does not support the booking or management of follow-ups (an appointment after the initial consultation). This leaves the responsibility for appointment management with the Secondary Care (hospital) provider regardless of how the initial appointment is requested. There is nothing preventing a

---

[17] An API provides a way for computer systems to talk to each other so that the information is shared without the need for humans to engage in the process.

secondary care organisation modifying the appointment date once it has been requested.

A further challenge with ERS is that demand is outstripping availability and patients are unable to access appointments within a reasonable timeframe. The traditional outpatient model has now shifted to virtual consultations and a 'channel shift' is occurring due to the COVID-19 pandemic.

Following a referral, the patient will be assigned an outpatient appointment in the PAS Module, where they will be seen by a specialist clinician (or one of their team)[18]. At this appointment, the patient will usually undergo some diagnostic tests or be referred for diagnostics related to their symptoms with a view to achieving a diagnosis for treatment.

Once the patient has a diagnosis and where appropriate, they will be placed onto a care pathway for treatment. This may result in a pending hospital admission requiring some form of advanced observation, treatment or follow-up surgical procedure. Pending admissions are managed through the PAS waiting list functionality. Waiting lists are often the centre of media and parliamentary scrutiny due to the fact that waiting list demand is often far superior to the resources able to meet the demand. For this reason NHS England set an operational target in 2014 that no patient should wait longer than 52 weeks for treatment in the NHS (the 52 week wait).

Emergency Visits (A&E)

A&E hospital visits are considered an accelerated version of the above process. A patient is referred directly for treatment either

[18] The NHS operating framework and constitution states that all patients should begin treatment within 18 weeks of the referral (this is also known at the Referral To Treatment rule or RTT).

by themselves, their carer or through an emergency response (ambulance, helicopter etc.). These referrals are categorised as an 'Emergency Referral' and once the patient is admitted they are managed using the same process as a GP referral.

Once in the Emergency Department, 'walk-in' patients are registered onto the Emergency IT system or module and triaged by a nurse. If the patient could be treated elsewhere the nurse will divert the patient to a more appropriate care provider such as the GP or an out of hours location. In the event the patient requires mental health or social care support the patient is referred to the appropriate mental health or social care provider.

Emergency visits will either result in an admission to hospital for specialist care, or treatment in the department with a subsequent Emergency Department discharge. Once discharged, a document is sent to the GP within 24 hours (the Emergency Discharge Summary) so that the GP can manage any follow-up care. If the patient is admitted they are then treated as an inpatient and managed by the appropriate hospital team until discharge is possible.

Chapter Seven – Outpatients and Day-Cases (Elective Admissions)

An outpatient is a patient who attends the hospital to receive treatment without staying overnight. Outpatients are generally managed in a clinic environment using appointment slots and relevant diagnostic scheduling. An outpatient appointment is the first point of contact with a clinical specialist following a GP referral.

When a patient attends their outpatient appointment, they will discuss their symptoms with the clinician who will make decisions on the required follow-up diagnostics/treatment. In some outpatient clinics patients are expected to have a set of pre-defined observations completed prior to the outpatient clinical consultation. These are usually performed before the consultation takes place so that the clinician can review the results (such as X-rays, weight, blood pressure, etc.). All of these activities are recorded on the EHR system in the form of diagnostic orders, with the results feeding into the associated result module for review. Once the results are available, the clinician can make a decision on the best form of treatment for the patient.

Outpatient appointments are also used for follow-up care after a patients' hospital admission or elective surgery. These follow-up appointments are used to determine the condition and wellbeing of the patient and to monitor the progress of the patient following any surgery or clinical intervention.

During the outpatient consultation, the clinician will decide on the best course of treatment. This may mean ordering further diagnostics using the Order Communication module in the EHR system. Once these diagnostics are ordered the clinician will review the results of these diagnostic tests and formulate a treatment plan. A treatment plan may include an option for surgery, minor treatment, some medication or therapy.

Almost all of the activities above can be captured electronically and will make use of the Scheduling, Documentation, Observations, Order Communication and Results Review modules of the EHR system. In some cases (such as diabetes) patients can be prescribed an 'app' for their smart-phone so that they can be monitored remotely. This 'channel shift'[19] in patient management is likely to continue for some time as hospitals make further use of technology. The use of video should be considered as a primary, rather than secondary method of outpatient consultation for some types of patients as this reduces travel, improves convenience and reduces the capacity challenge for care providing institutions. Due to COVID-19 this kind of care is becoming the new standard as individuals are unable to travel because of lockdown or shielding restrictions.

At this time, most hospitals will send a patient an outpatient appointment letter or an SMS link to their appointment. This correspondence will include a special barcode/link that the patient can use to check-in to their outpatient appointment. EHR systems include a check-in system that enables the patient to inform the outpatient clinic that they have arrived and large screens are used in the clinic to inform the patient which room they will be seen in by the clinician. The more advanced check-in systems allow patients to be managed between multiple floors and support the configuration of tasks to be completed prior to seeing the doctor. This technology streamlines the outpatient experience, reduces the 'shouting' required for patients to be seen and allows all of the required dependent clinical activities (such as X-rays and diagnostics) to be completed prior to the consultation. More advanced workflows include the use of the SMS link to carry out a virtual outpatient appointment which

[19] A channel shift is the provision of the same service using a different approach (such as digital).

may also include a telephone conversation (rather than a video) option.
As well as outpatient treatment, consultants also schedule day-cases, day-surgery or 'to come in' attendances. Day-cases are scheduled for minor operations and procedures that only require an admission to hospital during the day with the expectation that the patient will be discharged on the same day. It is often better for patients to be 'in and out' of hospital rather than to stay in hospital and potentially catch a hospital-acquired infection that could lead to serious complications.

Day cases are scheduled using the EHR theatres module with the appropriate theatre, staffing, equipment and timing to complete the procedure. Once completed, the theatres module is updated with the associated operation note and all medical equipment is checked back into the system to ensure that no equipment is missing.

As the NHS transforms outpatient services, the scheduling and management will be controlled by the patient through the provision of patient accessible apps. These apps provide the patient with a full schedule of their appointments, enable the patient to change their appointment, view the appointment letter and offer digital alternatives to travelling to the hospital (such as video consultations). Due to the complexity of managing scheduled appointments and the limited interoperability of PAS Modules, the full adoption of this concept will take some time to deliver to the healthcare sector.

This nirvana of patient experience is not common in the NHS but has changed following the COVID pandemic. I cover this in more detail in Chapter Twenty-Three – COVID-19.

Chapter Eight – The Patient Admission

Once it has been agreed that a patient should be placed into hospital the patient becomes an 'inpatient' and they are 'admitted'. There are generally two types of hospital admission, elective and an emergency admission.

Patients are admitted through the elective process when they have been previously seen by a clinician at an outpatient appointment. During the outpatient appointment, the patient discusses their treatment options with the clinician and an elective admission is scheduled. An elective admission is required for specialist treatment or surgery which necessitates a stay in hospital. Day cases are covered in Chapter Seven – Outpatients and Day-Cases (Elective Admissions).

An emergency admission occurs when a patient presents to the hospital through an emergency care pathway. This is usually through the Emergency Department (A&E) but can also be via an emergency referral from another hospital, in cases where patients deteriorate and require specialist urgent treatment or for rare (infectious) diseases.

Whilst in hospital, several processes are used to manage the care of the patient. Each process is designed so that patients receive optimal care depending on the severity of their illness. For example, in an Intensive Care Unit (ICU) the patient will receive one-to-one nursing care, continuous observation and have strictly managed and controlled drug prescriptions. On other wards this process is different, with nursing provided based on the needs of the patient demographic/criticality of the ward.

The management of a hospital ward must follow strict national guidance. National guidance for ward management includes ensuring that patients are not placed into areas with differing sexes (same sex wards), that wards are cleaned to the highest level, patients with infections are isolated appropriately and that there is a correct number of nurses on the ward for each shift depending on the level of sickness/acuity of the patients on the ward.

These processes are managed by a hospital coordination team and a ward management team which are responsible for auditing the wards (ideally on a per-shift basis) to ensure that all of the standards are being followed. In most hospitals, wards are managed by clinical speciality, for example urology wards, oncology (cancer) wards, renal wards etc. This approach ensures that clinicians keep their patients together and reduces the travel required to care for their patients.

From a technology standpoint, these processes can be automated into an admission, ward and bed management system (the PAS module, bed management module, infection control module and staffing level module). Modern EHR solutions include a ward and bed management solution as part of the PAS Module. This solution provides visibility on the demands of beds, the location of the beds, any alerts or activities outstanding for the patients on the ward and the likely discharge date for the patient.

Digital hospitals tend to use electronic whiteboards (touch-screens) on the ward to digitally display the status of each patient. These screens replace the legacy 'whiteboards' and marker pens that are used daily to display who is on the ward and the status of each patient on the ward at-a-glance. Whiteboards are used to track activities that are required or due to assist the patient being discharged from the hospital, assisting with hospital bed management.

During a stay in hospital there are several routines that are managed on the ward. These routines are;

- **The ward round** – is where the doctors, nurses and other health professionals visit every patient on the ward to discuss the status of the patients care and any further tests, treatments or medications required for the patient during their stay in hospital. At this time decisions are made on the patient's ability to go home (be discharged), the care package required for them to go home and any further follow-ups required following their admission. A mixture of electronic notes, referrals and orders are made during this process to progress the patient admission. In teaching hospitals this process is often supported by junior doctors who document the activities in the EHR on behalf of the leading (more senior) clinician.

- **The observation round** – observations are used to track the 'vital signs' of the patient throughout their stay in hospital. Vital signs include measurements such as heart rate, oxygen levels and blood pressure. Most hospitals in the UK use an Early Warning Score system that provides a score of the patient's current observations and these are captured and trended electronically using the observation module of the EHR system. Once captured, the measurements are calculated into a score to determine whether the patient is deteriorating, stabilising or improving.

- **The board round** – this is where staff stand by the whiteboard on the ward, discussing each patient and the status of activities required to progress the patient's care or to support their discharge. The outcome of the board round is the assigned ownership of tasks and activities to ensure that the patient's care is progressed appropriately. This is usually managed by a collaboration of therapists, doctors and nurses on the ward.

- **The drug round** – is where patients are given their medications. This process is completed using the prescribing module of the EHR system and patients are identified using Positive Patient Identification (PPID) prior to the administration (taking) of drugs during the drug round. In advanced digital hospitals, each bed on a ward will have a bedside drug cabinet that will only unlock (dispense) the drugs at the appropriate time for administration (giving the dose). These cabinets are also used for stock control, thus reducing the wastage in hospital prescribing.

- **The phlebotomy (blood test) round** – routine blood tests are taken for specific patients on the ward at given schedules throughout the day. Patients are Positively Identified (PPID) as the blood is taken and electronic barcodes are placed onto the blood sample bottles for identification in the laboratory module of the EHR system. These blood results are then electronically fed into the EHR system and the digital whiteboard system so that the alerts and activities are kept up to date and the appropriate notifications are displayed on the board.

- **The treatment round(s)** – although not strictly a formal part of hospital process, the treatment round is for all the other specialities that support patient care in hospital. These are the therapists and other disciplines that support patients to get back to a normal way of life following their admission.

- **Catering round(s)** – it is common for catering staff to visit the wards on a routine basis to collect food choices and deliver meals to patients. Modern EHR systems allow patients to order food at the bedside, providing the ability to record any allergies and their meal preferences.

Whilst in hospital it is common for patients to be transferred between care providers. These transfers generally occur for patients with co-morbidities, for example a patient may be transferred between a general medical ward to a renal ward if the patient presents with differing symptoms which are then diagnosed as a potential renal failure. Transfers are requested by the clinical staff and updated on the Patient Administration System (PAS). A porter is then called to execute the transfer (move the patient to the new ward) and the patient's care then continues under the renal team on the renal ward.

Chapter Nine – Discharge and Clinical Coding

Once the patient is better and fit to leave the hospital the patient is ready for discharge. Discharge is the process used to get the patient out of the hospital to the most appropriate discharge location. It is important that patients are discharged from hospital as soon as possible so that they can continue their recovery in their most comfortable surroundings. Discharging a patient early reduces the likelihood of a hospital acquired infection and improves the wellbeing of the patient.

Patient discharge is important due to the increasing pressures on the healthcare system; demand is outstripping supply for hospital beds. Discharge should only be considered if the patient is not going to be admitted again for the same condition. Readmissions cause a negative cycle for the care system and therefore when patients are discharged, they need to be discharged with the appropriate care package so that it is unlikely they will readmit in the future.

At times, discharging a patient from the hospital can be a complex process. Some patients may require modifications to their home, specialist equipment or in some cases rehoming. These kinds of issues often cause bed blockages in the hospital where patients who are fit to go home are unable to be discharged from hospital as they do not have a safe destination. It is not uncommon for NHS hospitals to pay for private beds to accommodate the demand for healthcare services.

A lot of work is being completed across the care economy in the UK to improve the relationship between healthcare providers, community services, social care services, emergency care and general practice (strengthened by the government policy for Integrated Care Systems). There are also discussions ongoing regarding the provision of 'care hotels' for patients to be moved at discharge to reduce the pressure on hospitals, allowing hospitals to deliver increased volume of patient care and for social issues to be resolved outside of the hospital setting.

Social care is statistically one of the biggest challenges when discharging complex patients. As social care is controlled by the Local Authorities (LAs, Councils) and healthcare is delivered by the NHS collaboration can be a challenge. This is primarily due to competing budgetary pressures and the continued reduction of funding available to LAs. For that reason, some hospitals are obtaining licenses to provide social care in an attempt to improve the collaboration with social services and reduce costly delays in the discharge process.

As mentioned above, discharge management should begin from the point of admission once a diagnosis and the social circumstance are understood. This may involve a multi-disciplinary care team coming together to understand the patient's treatment, likely time to recovery and the time it takes to set up the necessary requirements for a patient to be safely discharged home. The use of technology such as video conferencing (Multidisciplinary Team Meetings, MDTs) and multi-disciplinary task management supports a holistic approach to discharge. This is where many EHR systems fall short as they tend to be very 'inward' looking or care setting/hospital centric. A modern EHR solution needs to support 'system wide' collaboration and cross the boundaries between hospitals, general practice, community and social care settings.

Similar to inpatient management, discharge is managed using the PAS Module of the EHR System, the task management module, care planning module, clinical documentation, diagnostics and prescribing modules. All of these modules are reviewed and updated together to manage the discharge of the patient, ensuring the patient is sent home with the correct prescription, known as the To Take Out (TTO) prescription and the appropriate follow-up either in outpatients or in the community, is scheduled.

When a patient is discharged, they should be given a copy of their discharge letter/summary which is a document outlining the treatment and follow-up care they are to receive following their admission to hospital. This discharge letter should also be sent to the GP within 24 hours of discharge.

In 2016, NHS England launched the Transfer of Care initiative[20], an initiative which aims to standardise the discharge letter for patients. The aim is for all discharge letters to follow the Academy of Medical Royal College (AoMRC) Professional Standards[21] for the structure of medical documents. Once the discharge letter is completed it can then be sent electronically to the GP using the Message Exchange for Health and Social Care (MESH) messaging system. MESH uses structured electronic communications to send the discharge to the recipient. The target is for all discharge letters to be sent using MESH by 2018. Due to technical difficulties this ambition has yet to be achieved but is expected to accelerate across "First of Type" (FOT) adopters in 2021.

Following the patient's admission, the patient episode is 'coded' so that the cost of the admission can be reclaimed by the hospital. Coding the admission is carried out by the clinical coding team of the hospital. This team is responsible for identifying the activity that took place during the admission and assigning the most appropriate (cost) codes to the episode of care.

---

20 https://digital.nhs.uk/transfer-of-care-initiative

21 http://www.aomrc.org.uk/wp-content/uploads/2016/05/Standards_for_the_Clinical_Structure_and_Content_of_Patient_Records_0713.pdf

Clinical coding is a complex discipline where specialist knowledge is required to understand the correct codes to be applied to a visit depending on the patient's co-morbidities and the treatments received whilst in hospital. It is often difficult to ascertain the primary diagnosis for a patient visit due to the maturity of some older digital systems and this is where the clinical coders' expertise is required. The primary job of a clinical coder is to find the correct information, identify and code the correct diagnosis and capture the most appropriate procedures performed during the patient admission. As the majority of hospitals have yet to digitalise the patient notes this often means scanning a significant amount of paper to find the information.

Coding is essential to the health system as it allows information to be centrally aggregated and analysed. Having a consistent identifier for the patient episode allows for episodes to be funded according to the activity that took place during the hospital stay. The use of coding also supports secondary use cases such as tracking the quality of care, ensuring that patients receive consistent outcomes across the health service and that subsequent audit can be carried out across the healthcare system.

A clinical coder will make use of the entire EHR system to understand the admission and the clinical coding module is then used to record the appropriate diagnosis and procedure code(s). The clinical coding module enables the coder to search a clinical term store for the most appropriate diagnosis (International Statistical Classification of Diseases (ICD10)) or procedure code (Classification of Interventions and Procedures (OPCS)).

The strategic national standard for coding in the NHS is the Systematised Nomenclature of Medicine (SNOMED). Although this is the preferred standard many NHS Trusts do not have a coding system or EHR that supports this standard so the use of ICD10 and OPCS is still used for costing/financial purposes. As the digitalisation of the health service continues, the capture and use of SNOMED at the point of care (by the clinician) will become more mainstream, enabling the automation of clinical coding and reducing the cost of coding to each NHS organisation. In an attempt to resolve the maturity gaps, NHS-Digital have progressed the deployment of a terminology server which can be used to progress the adoption of SNOMED in NHS IT systems. More information on the NHS Terminology server can be found here: https://digital.nhs.uk/services/terminology-servers.

Chapter Ten – Community Care

Community Care is the service used to provide care outside of the hospital. Community services are services such as out-of-hospital care hubs, home wards, home visits and general practice. The delivery of enhanced community care is a significant aspect of the healthcare strategy for the UK. Effective community teams can reduce the requirement for further patient admissions to hospitals, providing a care prevention and support service.

The management of community services is different to how care is managed within hospitals. On discharge, a patient will be referred to the community services for follow-up and then placed on a community care rota. Community teams consist of nurses, doctors and therapists who are able to visit the patient or provide care at a more convenient location outside of the hospital. An example of a community service is the community midwifery team that is responsible for pre and post-natal support, ensuring safeguarding and wellbeing of mother and baby. Community care may also provide (depending on where you live) nursing support to schools for vaccinations or other medical needs.

Since the Government disbanded Primary Care Trusts in 2013, the delivery of community services has been handed over to other care-providing organisations (such as newly established community trusts, secondary care or mental health organisations). In some cases, the delivery of community care has been privatised, with organisations such as Virgin Care becoming responsible for the delivery of community services.

Community Healthcare is regulated by the Care Quality Commission (CQC) in four categories:

- Community Healthcare – provided to people in their homes, schools or through a care hub.

- Community Learning Disability Services – who assist with patients learning difficulties.

- Community Mental Health Services – for people with mental health needs.

- Community Substance Misuse Services – for people who misuse drugs or alcohol.

Digitalisation of community services is a challenge due to limited pervasive country-wide connectivity. Therefore, community services require a mobile solution that works both online (connected) and offline (disconnected), often in areas with limited or no network connectivity. The digitalisation of community service patient encounters is managed by some organisations using a paper transcription process with care workers electronically transcribing from paper 'back at base' following a busy day delivering care in the community. This is a false economy and reduces the efficiency of community staff, especially considering the modern capabilities of mobile devices.

The choice of mobile device in the community setting should be carefully considered as staff may travel to potentially unsafe areas with high rates of crime. To support the effective delivery of community care, the teams require a synchronisation-based IT system that allows the care workers to download their patient rota (and case-notes) before an encounter. This allows the care worker to record the details of the encounter at the point of care, with the related information. Following the visit, the information should then automatically be fed to a centralised system when the care worker is connected.

Community rotas are complex and need to understand service dependency, staff availability and shift patterns. These rotas are managed on a daily basis to ensure that the appropriate care is provided in the community at the most appropriate time. It is common for community services to manage 'virtual wards'. These are community-based wards of patients who are at home but who still require consistent, regular care. Due to the above requirements, community IT systems have often struggled to meet the evolving needs of community services and therefore it is common place for community teams to make use of additional mobile 'e-form' systems as well as their community EHR.

Community care also includes general practice and social care. General practice and community services are one of the major benefactors of the 'failed' National Programme for IT (NPfIT). Social care is still considered behind the curve on digitalisation and is only just adopting the use of the NHS Number. Due to NPfIT, almost all general practice and community services have EHR systems and are therefore using national coding standards (moving from Reed codes to SNOMED). This digital maturity has led to the GP systems becoming the 'source of truth' for the patients' record, connecting to the national IT services. The National Programme for IT (NPfIT) is covered in Chapter Sixteen – National Systems and Services.

A drawback to the NPfIT was the lack of interoperability requirements defined as part of the procurement and contracts. NPfIT was formed on the premise that 'one size fits all'. This lack of strategic prudence led to 'closed systems' and unresponsive suppliers. These systems are now beginning to open up as the expectation of interoperability is now common practice. Unfortunately, the lack of interoperability has led to fragmented workarounds in clinical practice and many a frustrated clinical worker.

Chapter Eleven – Out of Hours, Emergency, 111 and London Ambulance

Out of hours, Emergency Care, 111 and the London Ambulance Service as well as the 999 service are all linked together in a complex network of referrals, 'handshaking' and digital system integration. This process begins with non-emergency symptoms or an emergency that results in an ambulance or helicopter Emergency Department (ED, A&E) admission.

In a non-emergency scenario, emergency care in the UK begins with the use of the NHS 111 service. NHS 111 is the non-emergency number used to access NHS services, it is staffed by medically trained advisors, doctors and nurses. Using this service, patients are triaged and referred to the appropriate care provider.

NHS 111 can refer patients to urgency care centres, out of hours GPs, or if appropriate, an ambulance can be requested. NHS 111 is a telephone screening service with integrated access to the computer systems at urgent care centres, enabling patients to be referred with clinical details transferred by the telephone service. Unfortunately, 111 and urgent care centres are not always connected electronically to hospital Emergency Department IT systems.

Once the patient is triaged by NHS 111, the service will determine if there is a requirement for the patient to visit an urgent care centre. If considered appropriate, NHS 111 will transfer the details and symptoms from the NHS 111 telephone call, adding the patient to the urgent care centre 'to arrive' list. Using this information, the urgent care centre will prioritise the patient. In the event that a patient requires emergency care an ambulance can be requested by the NHS 111 service.

On the decision to transfer the patient to the Emergency Department the urgent care centre can transfer the details of the visit electronically. This allows the Emergency Department team to prepare for the emergency visit. It is possible for urgent care centres to transfer patients using an ambulance, helicopter or request the patient transfer themselves using their own transport mechanism.

The use of ambulances is now stringently managed by the ambulance service. Ambulances now have Global Positioning System (GPS) trackers and handover to the Emergency Department is strictly measured to ensure ambulances are used as efficiently as possible. Ambulances are managed by a Computer Aided Dispatch (CAD) system which provides an integrated mapping experience for call-handlers and also allows routine ambulatory tasks such as patient transport. The ambulance service (in London) uses a digital pin (4-digit code) system. A unique pin is generated for each emergency call and a corresponding pin is generated for the receiving hospital.

Digital pins are exchanged by the ambulance service and the Emergency Department at the point of patient handover. These pins are then entered into the ambulance tracking system to measure the time taken for handover. The pin codes are then used to determine how long the handover was and, if there was a delay, who was responsible (and subsequent financial penalty if appropriate). The target handover time is 15 minutes from arrival at the Emergency Department to handover to the clinical team in the Emergency Department.

Emergency Departments are measured using a four-hour patient waiting time target. This target is in place so that patients do not have to wait too long to receive care. Due to the increasing demand and complexity of patients visiting the Emergency Service, achieving this target is extremely difficult. To reduce the demand, patients are triaged by a triage nurse in the Emergency Department to prevent unnecessary emergency admissions.

Triage information is captured in the Emergency Department module of the EHR system (using an electronic form) and the four-hour wait time is calculated from the point of arrival to the point of discharge. The electronic documentation captured during an Emergency Attendance is called a Casualty Card (CAS Card – a detailed pictorial and narrative description of the patient condition at the point of attendance).

Emergency departments tend to be split into different sections or areas. These areas are likely to be:

- A Waiting Area – this is the area where patients wait to be triaged or seen by an Emergency Doctor.

- Majors – an area where patients with major injuries are treated, a major injury is something considered life changing or potentially life threatening.

- Minors – an area for treating patients with minor injuries such as gashes, cuts and major bruises. Some suspected fractures are also transferred to the minors area.

- Resuscitation (resus) – resus is the area where patients with major trauma or injuries arrive. These tend to be patients who have been brought into the hospital by a 'blue light' such as an ambulance or helicopter.

- Pre-Admissions (ward) – the pre-admissions ward is a holding area which enables clinicians to discharge patients from the Emergency Department (stopping the four-hour clock). This is generally a short-term holding ward used to care for patients until they are transferred to the specialist ward for treatment.

These areas are configured on the EHR system with an appropriate patient list. On each of these lists there is a set of alerts (icons) and visual indicators which show where the patient is against the four hour wait target they also alert the clinical teams to the availability of diagnostics and clinical observations.

As patients are triaged, they are processed through the Emergency Department until they are discharged or admitted to hospital. In all cases the emergency admission is considered a different episode of care to the inpatient (hospital) admissions. This is for compliance purposes but in some electronic systems this leads to a loss in diagnostic orders and blood results being transferred between episodes. It is therefore important that episodes are linked between the Emergency Department and the inpatient admission (even though from a costing and coding perspective they are different episodes of care).

The general flow from the Emergency Department is the decision to admit or decision to discharge. A decision to admit should be recorded as quickly as possible to notify the hospital management that a bed is required for the patient. It is preferred that a diagnosis be established as quickly as possible so that an appropriate specialist bed can be located in the hospital in the right department. Once the bed has been identified, the bed management system can then be used to hold the bed for the patient to be transferred from the Emergency Department.

Following an Emergency Department visit, an ED discharge summary document is produced. This document provides primary care (the GP) with the knowledge of the reason for the visit, any treatment, as well as the medication that was administered during the episode. As part of the NHS Digital Transfer of Care (TOC) initiative it is expected that discharge summaries are communicated with primary care within 24 hours of the visit to the Emergency Department.

Chapter Twelve – Interoperability Primer

Health Level 7 (HL7)

Healthcare interoperability has been a fundamental requirement since the creation of IT systems. Standalone systems, although better than paper, are dangerous in a clinical environment with transcription errors causing potentially fatal outcomes. Interoperability reduces these errors by using electronic communication (messages) between systems to ensure that the data captured in one clinical system is sent accurately to another. This is a complex process and requires a significant amount of testing before being deployed in a clinical environment. With interoperability maturing the argument of best of breed vs big EHR system diminishes as systems become more communicative and standardised, reducing the risk of a heterogeneous architecture.

The primary standard for systems interoperability in the healthcare market is a set of standards managed by HL7, with version 2 the primary standard published in 1989. HL7 is an international standards organisation responsible for the publication and management of interoperability standards. As a standards body HL7 is responsible for the publishing of several standards, the most common standards are;

- HL7 version 2.x – a legacy, well used text-based standard for healthcare system to system communication.

- HL7 version 3 – a standard which uses eXtensible Mark-up Language[22] (XML) to create a self-explanatory set of message structures. An evolution from HL7 2.x.

---

[22] XML is an internet standard for creating self-describing documents.

- Clinical Document Architecture (CDA) – a standard for clinical document exchanges, CDA provides a standard for sending documents such as discharge summaries between systems and care settings.

- Clinical Context Object Workgroup (CCOW) – an interoperability standard that enables different healthcare IT systems to interact with each other (for example share the same patient or clinical context).

- Fast Healthcare Interoperability Resources (FHIR) – a modern standard that uses internet technologies to share healthcare information.

The majority of healthcare systems in the market support HL7 2.x (version two is the major version, x is the minor version with v2.6 being the latest version) with an increased enthusiasm and adoption of FHIR now becoming the standard of choice.

HL7 version 2.6 is a plain-text based message format which is exchanged between IT systems to inform the systems of the information being added, updated or deleted. HL7 is a backwards compatible standard, so a system that supports version 2.6 should also support HL7 2.3.

Understanding HL7 can be difficult as it is complex and even more challenging to explain in a non-technical language. The easiest way to explain it is to imagine a radio conversation such as:

"This is Gary McAllister are you receiving? I am speaking English and the time now is 9 minutes past 11, I have just registered a new patient."

This is the introduction of the message and is contained in an opening 'segment', called the Message Header (MSH). A message header contains the details of the message, the time the message was generated and the transaction that took place (in this case it was an admit, transfer, discharge message (ADT) and a transaction type of A28 – a patient registration).

Following on from the Message Header, a number of other segments or details follow. In the case of a patient registration the radio message will continue.

"The patient I have registered is called Joe Bloggs. His date of birth is 15/06/1970. He is male, British and the local identifier for this patient is P123456."

This segment is called the Patient Identifier segment or (PID) and includes a person's demographics.

A sample HL7 message is outlined below (taken from the HL7 Wikipedia[23] page);

```
MSH|^~\&|MegaReg|XYZHospC|SuperOE|XYZImgCtr|20060
529090131-0500||ADT^A01^ADT_A01|01052901|P|2.5
EVN||200605290901||||200605290900
PID|||56782445^^^UAReg^PI||KLEINSAMPLE^BARRY^Q^JR
||19620910|M||2028-9^^HL70005^RA99113^^XYZ|260
GOODWIN                                  CREST
DRIVE^^BIRMINGHAM^AL^35209^^M~NICKELL'S
PICKLES^10000            W             100TH
AVE^BIRMINGHAM^AL^35200^^O||||||0105I30001^^^99D
EF^AN
PV1||I|W^389^1^UABH^^^^3||||12345^MORGAN^REX^J^^^
MD^0010^UAMC^L||67890^GRAINGER^LUCY^X^^^MD^0010^U
AMC^L|MED|||||A0||13579^POTTER^SHERMAN^T^^^MD^001
0^UAMC^L|||||||||||||||||||||||||||200605290900
OBX|1|NM|^Body Height||1.80|m^Meter^ISO+|||||F
OBX|2|NM|^Body Weight||79|kg^Kilogram^ISO+|||||F
AL1|1||^ASPIRIN
DG1|1||786.50^CHEST PAIN, UNSPECIFIED^I9|||A
```

23 https://en.wikipedia.org/wiki/Health_Level_7

An HL7 message contains multiple lines with fields within each line. Each field is separated by the '|' pipe character and fields within fields (sub-fields) are separated by the '^' character. For example `KLEINSAMPLE^BARRY^Q^JR` is the patient's full name split into sub-fields using the '^' character. To further complicate the standard, each field has a defined data structure. In the case of the name field the data structure is called the eXtended Patient Name (XPN) data structure. Data structures are used throughout the HL7 specification. A full definition of the data structures can be found in the HL7 specification obtained through purchasing a HL7 (UK) membership[24].

If you analyse the message you will see that each line contains details of the transaction. The first 3 characters in blue outline what the details contain. These segment identifiers are explained below:

- MSH – the message header, this segment explains the message formatting, the sending and receiving system, the identifier for the message, the time the message was created, the version of HL7 used to create the message (2.5 in this case) and the transaction that took place in the source system (This is an ADT^A01 – a patient admission).

- EVN – the event segment specifies the time of the transaction and the reasons for the transaction.

- PID – the Patient Identifier segment. This segment provides the demographics of the patient, including hospital number, NHS number (in the UK) and address.

[24] http://www.hl7.org.uk/

- PV1 – the patient visit segment, outlines the patient visit information such as the consultant, ward (location) of the visit, the time of the admission, time of the discharge etc.

- OBX – observation segment, contains observation details of the patient. In this example, it includes the height and weight inclusive of the measurement format used (meters and kilograms).

- AL1 – allergy segment provides details of patient allergies.

- DG1 – diagnosis segment specifies the diagnosis for the patient.

There are far too many segments and transaction types to outline the HL7 specification fully in this short book. A common list of transactions can be found in the table below for reference. This is not an exhaustive list but outlines the most commonly used transactions in a hospital setting.

Type	Transaction	Description
ADT[25]	A28	Patient registration (new patient added to system)
ADT	A31	Patient demographic update
ADT	A01	Patient admission
ADT	A02	Patient transfer (to new location or clinician)
ADT	A03	Patient discharge (patient has left the hospital)
ADT	A04	Patient registration (used for arrival messages)

[25] ADT – Admit, Discharge, Transfer

ADT	A05	Pre-admit (used for elective and outpatient appointments)
ADT	A08	Patient visit update
ADT	A11	Cancel admission
ADT	A12	Cancel transfer
ADT	A13	Cancel admission
ORM[26], OMG[27], ORU[28], OMI[29]	R01	Observation result message
ORM, OMG, ORU, OMI	O01	Order (for diagnostic tests, referral or prescription)
MDM	T01	Original document notification
MDM	T02	Document notification and content
MDM	T03	Document status change
MDM	T04	Document status change and content
MDM	T07	Document edit notification
MDM	T08	Document edit notification and content
MDM	T09	Document replacement
MDM	T10	Document replacement and content

In order for an HL7 message to reach a destination system, the message needs to be sent electronically from the sending system. Rather than the source system sending the message directly to

[26] ORM – Order, results message

[27] OMG – General clinical order message

[28] ORU – Unsolicited transmission of an observation message

[29] OMI – Imaging order

each destination system, a (Trust) Integration Engine (TIE) is used. A TIE sits between all of the systems and decides where to send each message. For example, a patient registration (A28) will need to be sent to every system that is interested in the patient's demographics.

The diagram below shows the position of an integration engine in a patient registration communication (although the same applies for all healthcare transactions).

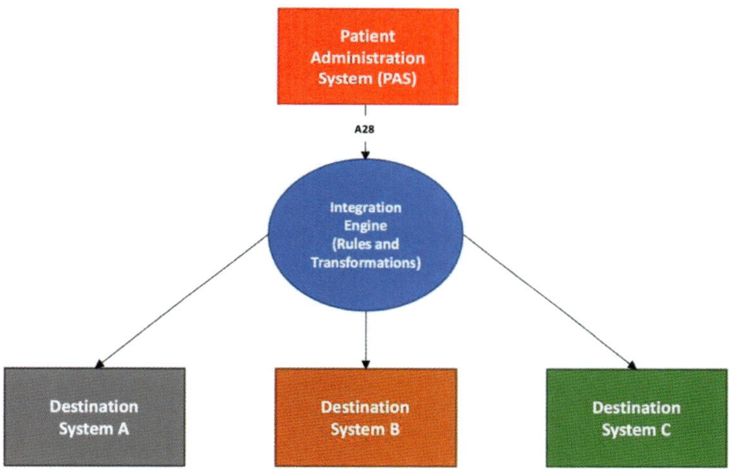

The TIE is the communication hub that receives all of the messages from the sending system and forwards the communication to the appropriate destination system(s). An integration engine is responsible for analysing the message content, deciding where the message needs to go to, changing the message structure if required and then sending the message to the destination system(s). An TIE removes the need for each source system to know where the destination system(s) live. All of this information is configured in the integration engine and can be managed centrally. This approach is known as 'PUSH' messaging as the message is sent from the source system to the destination system(s) once the transaction is completed in the source system.

Unlike HL7 2.x, HL7 v3 and FHIR are newer but less adopted standards. This is due to the history of use and implementation of HL7 v2.x. HL7 v3 progresses the communication standards into more of a descriptive, workflow-orientated set of structures known as the Reference Information Model (RIM). RIM structures HL7 into a set of domains that are workflow orientated and enables messages to encapsulate the information required to carry out an activity as part of a workflow design.

Fast Healthcare Interoperability Resources (FHIR)

FHIR is the latest standard in Healthcare Interoperability and the standard that everyone is excited about. The reason for this is that FHIR uses standard internet technologies to share and secure[30] information, reducing the need for proprietary communication protocols. As FHIR adopts standard internet technologies it is easier to work with and consume from a receiving system perspective, enabling the creation of modern 'apps' without reengineering the underlying system(s), reducing future engineering costs.

To understand FHIR, imagine that every patient's details are accessible via a website. For example, to get the details of a patient you would type the following address into an internet browser https://www.patientdetails.co.uk/patient/P123456. Once requested via the internet browser you then receive a specially formatted document that can be used by the destination system to consume the patient's details. This is the approach that FHIR uses and it is known as Representational State Transfer (REST). It enables the easy consumption of information across systems that are deployed using internet technologies.

---

[30] Smart on FHIR is a technology stack that supports the use of OAuth and FHIR.

Unlike HL7 v2.x one of the benefits of FHIR is that it can reduce the repetition of the storage of data. FHIR is a query-driven interoperability standard and therefore the destination systems can use the source information at the point of care without copying (duplicating) the information to a local data store. FHIR also supports the creation, update and removal of data in the source system using internet technologies so it is not necessary to duplicate functions across healthcare IT systems. As the standard evolves, we expect FHIR to adopt self-describing user interface and workflow additions so that healthcare systems can generate and consume specialist functions from other systems, reducing the time and effort for system communication.

The FHIR specification (at version 4) is split into 5 organisational levels with each Level utilising and enriching the previous level below:

- Level 1 – Basic framework, provides the description of data-types and the organisational structure of FHIR.

- Level 2 – Provides the expectations when implementing the standard. Specifies the security, adoption, usage and information exchange design patterns.

- Level 3 – Adds real-world concepts to FHIR by introducing data structures and message flows that can be used for patient administration purposes (such as patient definition, organisation and other concept documents).

- Level 4 – Detailed patient record definitions and structures such as Allergy, Problem Record, Observations, Medication etc.

- Level 5 – Introduces more advanced "Reasoning" capabilities such as sharing decision rules.

More information on the FHIR specification can be found here: https://www.hl7.org/fhir/index.html

Integrating the Healthcare Enterprise (IHE)

IHE is an initiative created by the healthcare industry to focus on the resolution of specific healthcare information sharing problems. IHE splits problems into problem domains known as IHE profiles. Each profile is created with a specific clinical workflow and the workflow is then mapped to a set of domain-specific technology designed to solve the information sharing problem. Once a system implements this technology profile the system then becomes IHE compliant in the specified problem domain.

The One London LHCRE Programme is adopting IHE profiles for improving interoperability across the London region. Taking a problem orientated approach ensures that the complete clinical workflow and series of interactions are considered as part of the interoperability profile specification. IHE does not mandate the use of specific technology standards but takes well-known technology standards and adds a layer of specification rigour to ensure that they are used correctly to enforce a specific workflow.

A common IHE profile is the Cross Enterprise Document Sharing (XDS) profile. This profile supports the sharing of patient documents across organisations and is commonly used to share Picture Archiving and Communication System (PACS) images in the Digital Imaging and Communications in Medicine (DICOM) file format. XDS does not specify the type of documents that can be shared; however, the profile enables organisations to share documents in any format between organisations using cross-organisation information queries. This approach is becoming more popular and will allow local portals to share information across regions to create an NHS-wide virtual care record.

Open Electronic Health Records (OpenEHR)

OpenEHR is an EHR specification supported by a virtual community that takes a holistic view of defining an EHR system using information systems modelling principles. OpenEHR's approach has been accepted as an ISO standard for the specification of EHR systems[31], taking a layered approach to EHR system specification. The advantage of the adoption of OpenEHR is that once an IT system is built to OpenEHR principles it should be interoperable, with security, data and functionality all compliant to the standard.

OpenEHR is a difficult concept to understand but can be imagined as functional and non-functional specifications, called architypes, of an Electronic Health Record system. The documentation is written and specified in a format that is designed to enforce clinical best practice and is managed by a broad community of active clinicians.

In theory, you can auto-generate an EHR IT system using the OpenEHR specification(s) as the specifications are not technology dependent. OpenEHR specifies the entirety of an EHR system; from the security and audit specification, to logical data specifications and the recommended separation of information. OpenEHR is working on a specification format for clinical validation (safety) and workflow interactions. OpenEHR has a broad community of clinicians contributing to the clinical models contained within the architecture. The Clinical Knowledge Manager can be found at http://www.openehr.org/ckm/.

---

[31] https://www.iso.org/standard/50119.html

Chapter Thirteen – Portals and Population Health

In 2010, you couldn't go to a healthcare IT conference without a vendor selling the latest and greatest in portal technology. In a broad sense a portal is a gateway or alternative entrance to another world. In IT, a portal is a piece of software (usually a secure website) that enables access to one or many other IT systems using one of several technical mechanisms. In simple terms a portal should provide access to healthcare information from one or many sources, using a single login, in the most convenient and relevant way required by the healthcare or analytical worker.

Portals in a healthcare setting are leveraged for two purposes, 'direct patient care', used by clinicians in a patient care setting or 'secondary use'. The term 'secondary use' is a general term and relates to the use of patient data for purposes that are not directly related to patient care such as analytics or research. Each of these approaches have differing implications on information governance and patient consent. This is covered in more detail in Chapter Fourteen – Information Governance (IG) and Security.

A direct care portal pulls information from underlying IT systems into a set of information views that can be used to support the ability of the clinician to deliver patient care. For example, a large specialist healthcare organisation is likely to have many (even hundreds) of specialist healthcare IT systems. Bringing this information together results in a clearer view of information for the clinician who is treating the patient.

As well as bringing information together from lots of IT systems, a portal can be used to surface information from a large EHR system into 'speciality specific' views. This approach is required because large EHR systems provide so much functionality it is often difficult to consume without browsing between functions, which isn't the most efficient use of clinical time.

Academically portals leverage Enterprise Application Integration (EAI) techniques to integrate the data from the underlying information system into the portal. EAI is the unrestricted sharing of data and business processes among any connected application or data sources in the enterprise. To put this in healthcare terms, EAI is ensuring that all of the required patient information is available from all sources to support and automate the patient pathway.

An outcome of an EAI portal delivery will support the viewing and fulfilment of all the diagnostics, investigations and treatments required to provide the best possible care in a single view. The portal should also eradicate the duplication of login, information entry and business process.

The technical mechanisms that can be used to integrate portals are:

- User-interface integration – uses the existing user-interface (the screens that the user interacts with) and brings these together into a portal. This results in a 'controller' portal that has the ability to interact with the existing systems display ensuring that the required user-interface 'screen' is displayed from the underlying information systems at the right time in a process.

- Middleware "Interoperability" Integration – this is the most common integration mechanism and occurs using specialist pieces of software that connects the systems together. As discussed in Chapter Twelve – Interoperability Primer most healthcare systems provide an integration layer which can be accessed to connect systems together. This middleware allows portal vendors to add, update, read or delete information from a source system. Unfortunately, not all healthcare system suppliers provide good middleware interoperability which results in messy workarounds that are difficult to support but are the only option if the patient pathway is to be completely shared across IT systems.

- Data integration – takes a different approach by exposing the data directly to the portal by accessing the underlying data storage mechanism. Data integration is often the last resort as it results in cumbersome integration solutions. That being said, data-integration is often the only approach possible with some healthcare IT systems. This is because healthcare IT systems have evolved from legacy platforms and are not created to be 'open by design'. A mature approach to overcoming this problem is to create interoperable interfaces on top of existing healthcare systems.

As interoperability evolves portals should be seen as a means to an end for bridging healthcare systems and processes. Mature interoperability will allow information and processes to be brought together using natural 'open' interoperability. This may take some time to achieve but with organisations such as OpenEHR and HL7 beginning to standardise the specification of EHR systems and interoperability standards, open interoperability will become an integral part of healthcare digitalisation.

Portals are important to support the management of large populations of patients, especially when considering the challenges of the provider commissioning model described in Chapter One - The NHS Healthcare System. These challenges have resulted in the creation of Sustainability and Transformation Partnerships (STPs) and Systems Leaders, amalgamating the health service into Integrated Care Systems. With the creation of Integrated Care Systems and the division of the health service into regions of care there is a requirement for a population-based approach to the analysis and management of information. This analysis is provided through Population Health Management Systems or portals which provide a central hub of information, brought together to support the provision and delivery of patient care for a specified region.

With care brought together into regions an 'outcome' based approach to healthcare can be established, moving the health system away from reactive to proactive. A proactive approach focuses on the improvement of healthcare for an entire population rather than individual cases, ensuring a population has the ability to adapt to life's changes. For example, a population system may focus on the improvement of blood pressure and reduction in smoking, drug and alcohol consumption. The success of these initiatives can be measured by the decline or normalisation of health issues related to these measures. In order to establish the success of an outcome-based healthcare model, the care system will require the integration of data from primary, secondary and social care into a single Population Health Analytics portal. Population Health Analytics provide the ability for commissioners and care providers to understand and provision care more effectively and adapt care models so that the outcomes are measurably more successful.

Population Health Portals differ from localised or regional portals because some portals can pull information in real-time (without storing the data locally) whereas a population health system needs to understand and store the data. Understanding the data enables population health systems to produce consistent and correct analytical statistics. This introduces a layer of complexity into the integration of the IT systems because all of the information provided must use the same coding and measurement standards. It is common in population health systems for data to be integrated and normalised into a staging data repository with the appropriate coding and measurement standardisation being conducted prior to publishing the results to the population health portal. This normalisation process is time-consuming, expensive and complex and should never be underestimated as it always takes longer than you expect.

Once the standardisation of data has been achieved the Integrated Care System can use the data/analytic system to understand the local population health status. Once the analytics has been completed, the governance body can implement the appropriate public health initiatives, which in turn should reduce pressure on the health system (and in economic terms improve the productivity of the population which then improves the Gross Domestic Product[32] of the country).

[32] https://en.wikipedia.org/wiki/Gross_domestic_product

Chapter Fourteen – Information Governance (IG) and Security

IG is vital for the management of information and is a practice that all enterprises should use for the management of information policy, security and information risk management. As well as the management of information control, information governance defines the principles and management as to how information should be secured.

In the NHS, IG has been well-established for some time. This is evident due to the importance of Dame Caldicott's principles, originally published in 1997 and reviewed in 2013 and 2016, these principles set out what is required for the handling and sharing of patient information. With important legislation such as the Freedom of Information Act (2000), the Computer Misuse Act (1990), the Health and Social (Quality and Safety) Act (2015) and the Data Protection Act (2018), it is important that all organisations have robust governance, security and information management plans in place.

> During the COVID-19 pandemic the Secretary of State issued a Control of Patient Information (COPI) notice to NHS Digital to relax the information governance rules in order to protect public interest and improve the speed of the COVID-19 response[33]. This notice has been used throughout the NHS as a guiding principle to relax IG restrictions.
>
> Anyone using the COPI notice must keep an up-to-date log as to who they are sharing information with for COVID-19 reasons. The current notice expires on the 31st March 2021 and it is not clear whether these rules will be relaxed for the longer term.

[33] https://bit.ly/3qaRZIS

Information Governance in healthcare relates to all data and Information Security (IS), especially the storage of personal data, which includes both staff and patient data. In both cases, there must be a valid and justifiable reason for the storage and use of an individual's personal information and the access to that information must only be for legitimate purposes. A primary resource for the management of information in the NHS is the NHS code of practice for handling confidential information[34].

Information Governance is even more complex when you start including patient consent, safe haven and the principles of the Health and Social Care (Quality and Safety) Act. There is an expectation (by law) that information will be shared to the benefit of the patient and that the patient will be informed and must consent to the sharing of their information. This is all documented in the Dame Caldicott 3 review which was published in 2016 and updated in July 2017[35].

As well as patient consent, Information Governance in the NHS includes the concept of an Accredited 'Safe Haven' (ASH). An ASH is an approved location for patient data to be stored and linked (using a single identifier) from multiple sources for research purposes without patient consent. It must be noted that the information must be anonymised but can be traced back to the origin. For example, most NHS Patients have an NHS Number as described in Chapter Three – Identifying the Patient. This identifier can be used as a single identifier to bring information together into a central information store, link the data together and create an analytical database. All of this is covered under Section 251 of the NHS Act 2006.

---

[34] https://digital.nhs.uk/codes-of-practice-handling-information

[35] https://www.gov.uk/government/publications/review-of-data-security-consent-and-opt-outs

Dame Caldicott is the driving force behind Information Governance in the NHS. Caldicott originally published her six principles of governance in 1997, with a seventh principle added in 2013. Core to the 1997 report was a series of recommendations with the most prominent that every NHS Trust should appoint a clinical lead for Information Governance (a 'Caldicott Guardian') as a custodian of Information Governance. As well as appointment of a clinical lead, the report recommended the production of a national accreditation framework for Information Governance which was later developed as the Information Governance Toolkit (IGT). Since the 31st December 2016 the NHS Information Governance Toolkit (IGT) has been phased out with a Data Security and Protection Toolkit (DSPT) being developed to replace it. More information on DSPT can be found at https://www.dsptoolkit.nhs.uk/.

In most NHS organisations clinicians are too busy to take on the role of Caldicott Guardian full time so the position is given as additional Professional Activities (PA's). It is therefore common for NHS Trusts to appoint an Information Governance manager to manage the day-to-day Information Governance activities.

Information Governance – Key Roles

The prominent roles of Information Governance in the NHS are:

- National Data Guardian (NDG) – Dame Fiona Caldicott, the most senior Information Governance officer in the NHS and has been responsible for three key reports that have shaped Information Governance in the NHS.

- Caldicott Guardian – is a clinical role responsible for the management and governance of patient information.

The Caldicott Guardian is often the local organisational officer, providing advice to clinicians and staff inside an organisation who have common concerns with sharing and managing patient information. Caldicott Guardians are not required in Clinical Commissioning Groups (CCGs).

- Information Governance (IG) Manager – is responsible for the day to day (legal) management of IG and compliance within an NHS Trust, more broadly for all aspects of IG. The IG Manager provides advice and guidance to the Caldicott Guardian and enforces the strict rules in relation to Information Governance. An IG Manager has knowledge of the governance rules specific to the NHS.

- Information Security Manager – is a more technical role responsible for applying Information Security principles. Information Security experts require an understanding of Information Security technology architectures, principles and the application of Information Security Governance. Information Security is centred on the Confidentiality, Integrity and Availability (CIA) principles that state information should remain confidential until an authorised individual requests access, that there should be controls in place to ensure that the Integrity of information cannot be compromised by either a person or cyber threat and that every possible measure has been put in place to ensure the Availability of information is reliable and robust.

- Senior Information Risk Owner/Officer (SIRO) – on the 20th May 2008, Sir David Nicholson wrote to NHS Trusts to recommend the appointment of a board level person to take accountability for Information Risk management. The role is responsible for supplying the

Information Risk management statements in the organisation's Annual Report and the nominated board member must have the experience and background to warrant their appointment. The SIRO may also be responsible for signing Freedom of Information responses.

- Information Asset Owner(s) – the nominated owner of 'Information Assets' held within an organisation. An Information Asset can be physical (paper) or a digital information system. The information asset owner is responsible for warranting that their Information Asset is appropriately utilised (governed and managed) and fully exploited within an organisation.

These roles are supplemented by the General Data Protection Regulation requirement to have a Data Protection Officer (DPO) who is accountable for the application of Information Governance within an organisation. NHS Trusts must appoint a DPO in order to be GDPR compliant.

Caldicott Principles

The 1997 Caldicott Report contained six principles and sixteen recommendations for every NHS organisation. These recommendations were put forward so that all NHS staff are aware of the seriousness to keep healthcare information secure and confidential.

In 2013 the original six principles were updated with a seventh principle that expresses the importance of information sharing to patient care. The Caldicott principles are included in the NHS confidentiality code of practice which was produced in 2003[36].

[36] https://digital.nhs.uk/article/1200/Confidentiality

1. **Justify the purpose(s)** – the use and sharing of information should be fully justifiable, scrutinised, clearly defined and reviewed regularly by the Caldicott Guardian.

2. **Don't use patient-identifiable information unless it is necessary** – patient information should only be used if it is critical for the workflow. If identifiable data is not required it should be removed prior to the use of the information.

3. **Use the minimum necessary patient-identifiable information** – If patient-identifiable data is required and justified it should be the minimum needed to fulfil the requirement of use.

4. **Access to patient-identifiable information should be on a strict need-to-know basis** – access to patient identifiable information should only be provided to people who must have justified access to the information. Care should be taken to ensure that only the data items required are displayed to the person.

5. **Everyone with access to patient-identifiable information should be aware of their responsibilities** – all people with access to patient-identifiable information must be trained and informed of the importance of security and confidentiality of the information they are handling.

6. **Understand and comply with the law** – All handling of patient information must be lawful. People with access to information must have appropriate knowledge of the associated laws.

7. **The duty to share information can be as important as the duty to protect patient confidentiality** – patients may move between care providers and care settings. If a

patient does move between care settings, and it is in the patient's best interests, appropriate information should be shared to the benefit of the patient, thus improving the quality, efficiency and safety of patient care.

Data Protection Act (2018)

The Data Protection Act 2018 (DPA) is designed to protect personal data, defined as any information that is stored on a computer. DPA 2018 is the UKs adoption of the GDPR regulations into UK law.

Definitions

The DPA uses key definitions when discussing the use of, and sharing of data. As the health service digitalises and continues to share data it is important to understand the following definitions and the legal obligations of information sharing:

- **Data Controller** – a person or organisation who (either alone, or jointly, or in common with other persons) controls the purposes for which and the manner in which any personal data is, or is to be, processed.

- **Data Processor** – in relation to personal data, means any person or organisation (other than an employee of the data controller) who processes the data on behalf of the data controller.

- **Data Subject** – means an individual who is the subject of personal data.

More information on the Data Protection Act can be found at: https://ico.org.uk/for-organisations/guide-to-data-protection/

Fair Processing

As well as the above definitions, it is important that when personal information is shared or processed that this is carried out in a transparent and open manner. For example, a patient may have blood results captured during a hospital admission but may not expect or want that information to be visible to their GP.

The Data Protection Act stipulates that any processing of personal data should be communicated transparently to the data subjects (the patient in our case) so that any objections can be managed (usually resulting in an opt out procedure). In summary, the Data Protection Act states that if any data subject would object to the processing of their data then there is a legal breach of the Data Protection Act.

There are a number of exemptions to the Data Protection Act and these can be found at: https://ico.org.uk/for-organisations/guide-to-data-protection/exemptions/.

General Data Protection Regulation (GDPR)

GDPR is a European Union (EU) Directive that updates the previous 1998 data protection legislation. The purpose of GDPR is to make organisations more accountable for compliance as well as giving the data subject (the person) control over their information.

The original Data Protection Directive was adopted in 1995. The issue with the Data Protection Directive 1995 was that it was a non-binding directive, allowing each member state the option to choose how to adopt the recommendations within the Directive. This ambiguity led to different interpretations and laws being implemented across the EU member states. The UK Law covering the previous Data Protection Directive was the Data Protection Act 1998.

To unify these Laws the European Union published GDPR on the 27th April 2016 with the enforcement date being the 25th May 2018. The adoption of GDPR was passed through government with Royal assent on the 25th May 2018, updating the parliamentary Data Protection Bill, and the previous Data Protection Act 1998 to a 2018 revision.

The Data Protection Bill provisions the adoption of GDPR in to UK law (the Data Protection Act 2018), extending the coverage of the regulation to include law enforcement, national security, research and child protection data. As well as amendments to the types of data adopted within UK law, the Data Protection Bill adapts GDPR so that it conforms to exemptions previously covered in the Data Protection Act of 1998. National security is considered within the bill with appropriate amendments covering UK Law enforcement agencies, allowing access to data for law enforcement purposes.

A proposed change to the UK legislation is the Information Commissioners Office (ICO) will now be able to enforce a maximum penalty of £17m or 4% of annual global turnover.

Individual Rights

The primary focus of GDPR is the protection of the data subject's rights when it comes to storing and processing personal data. Each data subject has the following rights under GDPR.

- The right to be informed – people should be informed as to how their information is used in entirety. This should be provided using a clear privacy notice.

- The right of access – data subjects should have access to their data and any relevant supplementary information.

- The right to rectification – personal data should be rectified if it is incorrect or incomplete. Any sharing of the data with 3rd parties should also be rectified under the same process.

- The right to erasure – people can request that their data is erased. Healthcare is excluded from this regulation due to data being held for the benefit of public interest.

- The right to restrict processing – data subjects can restrict processing of their data if the data is deemed incorrect, is due to be erased, a processing objection has been made explicitly or if the data controller no longer needs the data.

- The right to data portability – allows data to be moved from one service to another without restriction and the degrading of the data.

- The right to object – people should be provided with the right to object to data processing at the first point of contact with the service. Objection relates to processing of data for marketing, research or public interest projects (such as profiling).

- The right not to be subject to automated decision-making including profiling – GDPR protects individuals from dangerous automatic decision making, ensuring that manual intervention is conducted at all automated decision points.

As well as individual rights, GDPR focuses on providing the data subject with enhanced control and interaction with their data. The regulation covers a number of additional key areas, these are summarised below;

- Consent – GDPR Enforces explicit consent from the data subject for the storing of their data. Consent must be given freely, specific for the purposes of use, informed and unambiguous. It is no longer acceptable for consent to be inferred from silence or auto-populated tick-boxes.

- Children – the regulation specifies that children must be 16 for their data to be processed lawfully. This regulation will be lowered to a minimum of 13 in the UK.

- Subject Access Requests – data subject access request responses must now be completed within a month, non-chargeable and only refused if deemed excessive. A full explanation outlining the rejection should be supplied and should be in place for complaints.

- Data Protection Officer – every organisation must appoint a data protection officer. Healthcare organisations are explicitly stated as requiring this role under Article 29 of the regulation. A data protection officer must report to the highest level of management in the organisation.

As well as the above, each organisation should ensure that each employee has full awareness of GDPR and that a full audit is conducted covering all sources of personal information. All privacy notices should be updated so that data subjects have awareness of the controls in place that support the secure use of their data.

The above may seem worrying and excessive when applied to Healthcare but thankfully the Data Protection Bill has this covered under the following guidance.

"Organisations that process special categories of data on public interest grounds will be able to continue to do so."

Chapter Fifteen – Research Principles

Research within the NHS is governed by the Department of Health research governance framework[37]. This framework sets out all of the guiding principles and governance required to successfully manage and control NHS research institutions and projects.

NHS research is classified into 5 management domains these being:

- Ethics – any research project should be reviewed by an independent ethics body to ensure that the safety and wellbeing of participants is considered in the research study. This involves the process of defining and agreeing consent from the research study cohort (subjects). All research projects should require ethics approval prior to any studies being conducted.

- Science – repetition or copying of previous studies or a study that is not of a sufficient quality is deemed unethical. A governance structure should be in place for independent scientific review of the research study to ensure that the approach and hypothesis are of scientific quality and are not a duplicate of previous studies.

- Information – all research carried out in the Healthcare sector should be for the benefit of the patients, users, care professionals, and the general public. Access to information and research outcomes relating to health and social care should be open and freely available to use.

---

[37] https://www.gov.uk/government/publications/research-governance-framework-for-health-and-social-care-second-edition

- Health, safety and employment – Any research that involves dangerous elements (such as medicine trials) must be carefully managed, reviewed and controlled. Health and Safety risk assessments and mitigations must be provided with the research grant request.

- Finance and intellectual property – the use of public funds must be within HM Treasury guidelines and any use of existing or potentially created intellectual property must be well understood prior to any research being conducted.

Information in the Health Sector is arguably the most personal and sensitive information that can be held on a person. That being said, research (analytics) is required to improve health processes, diagnostics, treatment, medicines and therapies. It is therefore important that health information can be used for secondary purposes (other than direct care, the primary purpose) to improve care services.

The principles regarding research in the NHS are strict and as a rule of thumb patient identifiable information should always be removed from data sources before the data is released, analysed or published. In cases this rule can be relaxed if the organisation has an Accredited Safe-Haven (ASH) status which allows a single patient identifier to be retained on the records for reverse identification.

To clarify patient identification principles, there are four known states for patient identifiable data;

- Anonymised – data is completely anonymised and it is impossible for the data to be traced back to the originating patient or data subject.

- Pseudo-anonymised – data is anonymised but an identifier is generated and associated with the original patient/participant record so that the information can be traced back to the original record via a uniquely generated identifier.

- Weakly-pseudonymised – data items such as an NHS Number or a postcode can be retained in the research data-set which may allow direct identification of the patient but without retaining the full identity of the record.

- Identifiable – the data is completely identifiable (this is not allowed for research purposes).

National Institute for Health Research (NIHR)

NIHR[38] was established in 2006 and is an organisation funded by the Department of Health to consolidate and improve healthcare research.

The creation of the NIHR enabled the Department of Health to move away from ad-hoc research funding schemes to a consolidated organisation which would place the NHS as a global leader in healthcare research. It is the mission of the NIHR to improve care by providing end-to-end research that will have an impact on patient care.

---

[38] https://www.nihr.ac.uk/

Part of the remit of the NIHR is to create and fund Biomedical Research Centres (BRCs) for academic healthcare organisations that have the capability to create, develop and translate biomedical research from theory into direct care benefit. At the time of writing there are a total of 20 BRCs across England with a total funding of £817m provided over five years. This funding is available from the 1st April 2017.

A full list of BRCs can be found at https://www.nihr.ac.uk/explore-nihr/support/experimental-medicine.htm.

More information on the NIHR can be found at https://www.nihr.ac.uk/.

Secondary Use of Data

Although the principles above apply to research, they also apply to all secondary use of data within a healthcare organisation. This adds overheads when using healthcare data for the purposes of operational reporting and healthcare commissioning. For example, Clinical Commissioning Groups (CCG's) receive Pseudo-anonymised data from the data controllers which means that the commissioners rely on the data being anonymised correctly without any adverse modification prior to delivery for analysis.

Chapter Sixteen – National Systems and Services

It would be difficult to write an introduction to Healthcare IT book without mentioning the highly-scrutinised history of national IT services. This chapter provides an overview of these services, a high proportion of which have delivered significant value to the NHS.

National Healthcare IT gained political and public notoriety with the establishment of Connecting for Health (CfH), formally the Information Authority. CfH was a government funded agency and formally a division of the Department for Health (DfH). CfH was responsible for the creation and the delivery of the National Programme for IT (NPfIT, the National Programme) a programme which aimed to create a centrally held patient record that connected all primary and secondary care organisations in England. Ironically, CfH (CfH) was formed on the 1st April 2005 (April fools' day).

The National Programme for IT was delivered using a concept of Local Service Providers (LSPs), structured geographically by region. Once awarded, these LSPs were contractually bound to deliver selected IT systems across each region.

One can only assume that the regionalised setup was to prevent national vendor lock-in. It was these contracts, supplier capability, a lack of national healthcare resource, change readiness and technical maturity that led to the collapse and restructure of CfH (now NHS Digital) and the National Programme for IT (NPfIT).

This book will not go into the mistakes that were made by CfH as they are well documented elsewhere. Instead, this book focuses on the successful outcomes delivered by CfH, most of which are still in use today and deliver huge value to the health service. Some noticeable successes are:

- A Health and Social Care Network (HSCN), previously N3, a network which connects all health care providers in the country. HSCN takes advantage of modern MPLS technology to allow faster speeds and more diverse service provision on the national infrastructure. A 'peer' network is still retained by NHS Digital.
- Delivery of an NHS wide email platform. At the time one of the largest email infrastructures on the planet. This platform has since been taken over by Accenture and now offers Instant Messaging, Document Collaboration and Mobile Device Management as part of the NHS mail platform.

  Following the NHS mail 'technology refresh' the service now sits on the Microsoft Office 365 platform (in the cloud) and provides access to Microsoft Teams, SharePoint and other 'App' based functionality available on Office 365.
- Creation of an NHS Number architecture, having a single identifier for patients is the envy of many care systems around the globe.
- Implementation of national systems into Primary and Community Care.
- Progressing and delivering digital imaging (Picture Archiving and Communication Systems) to the NHS.
- Creation of the Messaging Exchange for Health and Social Care. A platform that now processes millions of transactions every week between primary care, secondary care, pharmacies and will soon integrate with social care.
- A national referral system, enabling primary care to refer patients to secondary care electronically ('Choose and Book', now named the e-Referrals Service).

- A summary care record solution that enables vital patient information to traverse care settings.
- The Secondary Use Service, a solution that enables outcome data from secondary care to be used for analysis and statistical research.
- NHS Enterprise Agreement – a licensing deal with Microsoft and other vendors to provide operating systems, office products and security software / applications (free of charge). This agreement was reinvigorated in 2019 as an N365 agreement for the public sector (which is a discounted Microsoft licensing provision for the NHS).

The national programme for IT was an ambition that was way before its time. It was created at a time when Facebook was being built in Mark Zuckerberg's dorm room and Google was still gaining momentum against Yahoo. The iPhone didn't exist, we were still chasing Moore's law[39] (a theory that computing power doubles every year) and IT infrastructure was excessively expensive. It is difficult to imagine how the national programme would have turned out had it been more flexible on delivery methods, supplier selection and the software functionality (and roadmaps) available to customers.

There are too many national systems, services and standards to go into detail on each. The following list describes the most significant systems and platforms provided nationally by NHS Digital. These are grouped together in the same classifications as NHS Digital for accessibility. The full list can here reviewed here: https://digital.nhs.uk/services

[39] https://en.wikipedia.org/wiki/Moore%27s_law

IT Infrastructure

The following services are provided by NHS Digital and are classed as infrastructure services.

- Health and Social Care Network (HSCN), formally the NHS Network (N3) – the national network for the NHS was originally provided by British Telecom (BT) and connects primary and secondary care as well as accredited bodies (through the IG Systems of Choice accreditation). The N3 network has been replaced with HSCN, a more flexible network which uses modern networking technology (MPLS). Unlike N3, responsibility for HSCN has been devolved across the NHS (back to the consumers) and the current expenditure for connectivity will be passed to each organisation and reduced on a sliding scale between 2018 and 2023.

- NHS Mail – a communications platform which provides a centrally managed contact directory, email and Skype for Business. The upgrade to NHS Mail (NHS Mail 2) was awarded to Accenture and was built in 2016 with a roadmap to introduce SharePoint and Mobile Device Management to follow. This is now hosted on Microsoft Office 365 and provides access to Microsoft Teams, SharePoint and other 365 capabilities.

- Network Addressing – registering NHS internet addresses for example www.gstt.nhs.uk or www.nhs.net.

- Registration Authority and Smart Cards – the national programme created a secure access service and registration authority. This service allows users to be registered to a central repository (the Care Identity Service) and issued with a secure access card (a smart-card). Once issued these cards can be used to access systems such as spine compliant IT systems, primary care systems, community systems or the e-referral system. The ambition was that the registration authority would be used as a standard for application security across the NHS.

This service is progressing towards a virtual alternative with the view that staff may eventually obtain a 'virtual identity' or wallet which will allow them to access NHS services.

- Organisation Data Service (ODS) – a service to provide unique identifiers to NHS organisations for the purposes of data collection and interoperability.

The SPINE

This section interrupts the NHS Digital website classification for infrastructure due to the scale of the NHS SPINE service. The issue with adding the SPINE to the infrastructure section is that the spine is such a large architectural component.

The SPINE is aptly named as it provides the backbone of services which are used nationally and by local NHS IT services. According to NHS Digital the spine now consists of the following services:

- Personal Demographics Service (PDS) – a national service that provides a centralised demographic store for the purpose of issuing and validating NHS Numbers. The service also validates existing patients, assigning an NHS Number where these do not exist so that a single and reliable demographic record can be obtained by all NHS IT systems.

- Personal Spine Information Service (PSIS) – a national service that stores clinical information. It is unclear how much use this service has in practice and the documentation on this service is limited.

- Electronic Prescription Service (EPS) – a platform that stores patient prescription information and enables records to be sent between primary care and pharmacies, reducing the need for manual paper prescription processes.

- Access Control Service (ACS) or Care Identity Service (CIS) – provides the components that allow users to login to nationally accredited computer systems. ACS is also known as the Care Identity Service (CIS).

- Messaging Exchange for Health and Social Care (MESH) – a platform that allows automated messages (such as discharge summaries or laboratory results) to be sent between care organisations in real-time using structured information formats.

- Child Protection – Information Sharing Project (CP-IS) – a centralised record service for hosting information for 'looked after' children or children who are on a child protection plan. The service alerts emergency or 'out of hours' care settings that a 'looked after' child is in the department and provides the details of the patient's social care team. On attendance, the information sharing service will notify the social care team and allow both parties to see the last 25 visits to unscheduled care settings in England.

Primary Care

Below is a list of services provided by NHS Digital that support primary care (General Practice).

- E-Referral Service (ERS) – ERS supports the referral process from primary care to secondary care and is the only supported mechanism for primary to secondary care referrals. The system is integrated directly into the GP system and allows the GP to look-up appointments at local NHS service providers based on the patients need. The roadmap for ERS includes triage and pre-referral vetting tools so that GP referrals are correct and do not waste secondary care resources.

- General Practice Collections – used by NHS Digital to describe the grouping of data collection from primary care. Data collected from primary care is used for payments, the Care Quality Reporting Service (CQRS) and to inform government departments on GP activity. Information is extracted automatically from primary care either directly from the system supplier or through a local IT service provider (such as a Commissioning Support Unit). This information is extracted and sent to NHS Digital for processing and analysis.

Hospital and Community Care

The enforced use of national systems within secondary (acute) care is limited. This is mainly due to secondary care autonomy. It is common for secondary care to make regular use of the e-Referral Service (ERS) and the Patient Demographic Service (PDS) as well as a broad use of infrastructure services. As NHS Digital reconsiders the approach to hospital and community IT delivery, the enforced use of national IT services may change drastically. Below is a common set of services used within secondary and community care:

- Summary Care Record (SCR) – is a centralised patient record service hosted on the SPINE. Created and updated through General Practice IT systems, the summary care record holds current medications, known allergies or reaction data and the current patient demographic. The summary care record is usually directly accessible in secondary care through the emergency department IT system to support out of hours and emergency care.

- Secondary Use Services + (SUS) (Secondary Care) – SUS + was launched in April 2017 and replaces SUS. SUS+ is a secure data warehouse that collects activity information from secondary care which is then used for payment (by results), commissioning, healthcare development and improving NHS resource efficiency. SUS data is aggregated by separating hospital data into commissioning datasets grouped together using tools such as the Healthcare Resource Grouper[40] (version 4). The HRG groupers is an algorithm based tool that groups hospital episodes together based on a formula depending on the commissioning data set.

- National Casemix Office – designs and refines classifications that are used by NHS England to define healthcare activity. A casemix is a 'mix of cases (patients)' that is seen in a care setting from inpatient to outpatient to emergency care. Although initially focused on acute care the casemix office has recently defined and developed specialist service casemix activity classifications.

---

[40] https://en.wikipedia.org/wiki/Healthcare_Resource_Group

Notable Interoperability Projects

As well as infrastructure, SPINE and sector specific services, NHS Digital is responsible for the national interoperability strategy. This strategy has evolved from a centralised, contract management, data and budget strategy to a federated, standards-based approach. Federating interoperability, data storage and finances support each care region to adopt approved standards that will allow healthcare information to flow more readily. Federation also allows regions to integrate on their own terms, promotes a successful interoperability approach and allows each region to develop interoperability based on the local populations needs.

Through this new strategy, NHS Digital has opened up connectivity over the internet for testing their centralised and contracted services. A result of these changes is open access to the following interoperability projects.

- GP Connect – provides FHIR access to patient records stored at the GP. GP Connect is an interoperable set of FHIR Application Programmable Interfaces[41] (see Fast Healthcare Interoperability Resources (FHIR)). These APIs enable portals and other care applications visibility

---

[41] An Application Programmable Interface (API) is a set of autonomous services that an IT system can communicate with to improve digital processes, consume logic stored outside of the current system, as well as reduce human interaction and improve access to information that is stored elsewhere.

An example of this is the Google Maps system which is a managed Google service but is widely used by other applications (such as the City Mapper app) to provide access to a digital mapping service without the need to reproduce a mapping system.

of primary care data for the purposes of information sharing and workflow improvement.

- E-Referral Service APIs – the ERS APIs provide autonomous access to the national e-Referral system and enable consuming IT applications to interact with the e-Referral service to improve access to the referral details.

- SPINE Mini Services – allow simplified access to the SPINE services to improve application workflows, enabling access to the SPINE suite of APIs.

- National Record Locator Service – a service that provides the ability for shared care records to contact other care records to retrieve information about a patient using a national index (or record locator). A cross regional query service.

- Terminology Server – solution that provides access to IT systems to support the standardisation of the use of clinical terminologies. Provides a foundation for mapping SNOMED to ICD10 and a national platform for other terminology solutions (DM+D etc.).

Standards

NHS Digital through the Data Coordination Board (DCB, effective 1st April 2017) is responsible for national technology, data (collection and extraction), terminology, governance and implementation standards. These standards are important as they ensure safe, secure and effective application of digital technology in health.

The standards are broad and cover many domains of interest. There are literally hundreds of standards published on the NHS Digital website, each of which are relevant to a chosen domain.

Some of these standards are referenced throughout this book such as DCB0034 – SNOMED-CT or DCB0086 – Data Security and Protection Toolkit.

There are some standards though which stand out above the others, these are summarised below (in no particular order):

- DCB0160 / DCB0129 – the important risk standards for digital implementation and manufacturing. These standards ensure that risk is considered whilst adopting and creating digital solutions. Application of the standards result in a thorough risk assessment for the implementation and creation of all digital services being used for patient care. Key documents and processes that are implemented whilst adopting these standards are the risk management plan, clinical safety case, a hazard log, incident management processes and a board chaired by the Clinical Safety Officer (for either the organisation or the supplier) who is responsible for signing off the use or marketing of digital services. More information on DCB0160 and DCB0129 can be found here: https://bit.ly/2X4FvGk and https://bit.ly/3pI3Ii5.

- DCB1521 – Cancer Outcomes and Services Dataset, known as COS-D is the dataset used to measure cancer services across the NHS. It is common for the somerset cancer registry (a system developed in Somerset) to be used by care providers to capture the vast array of information needed to support the Improving Outcomes: A Strategy for Cancer (IOSC) plan.

- DCB1609 – Child Protection Information Sharing provides the integration of vulnerable children data into unscheduled point of care settings so that care providers and social services can work together to protect vulnerable children.

- ISB0092 – Commissioning Data Set (CDS), referenced previously in this book provides the information to NHS England on activity taking place in secondary care. The data in the standard supports billing and capacity management. As part of the COVID-19 response the CDS submission moved to a weekly process.

- ISB0149 – the NHS Number standard. A standard used for validating and adopting NHS Numbers in care settings.

- DCB0084 – OPCS classification of interventions and procedures. The coding standard used in operating environments to capture any diagnostic, therapeutic or surgery activity for a patient.

- DCB1596 – secure email standard, protecting the transmission and receipt of email to and from health and social care organisations. Requires certification to become part of the NHS email network.

- SCI0034 – SNOMED-CT the terminology standard used for classifying activity in direct care. Provides an nested framework for finding and then coding episodes of care.

There are far too many standards to summarise them all, the full list can be found on the NHS Digital website. https://digital.nhs.uk/data-and-information/information-standards/information-standards-and-data-collections-including-extractions/publications-and-notifications/standards-and-collections.

Chapter Seventeen – LHCRE, Shared Care Records

On the 23rd May 2018 NHS England published the intent to create a set of Local Health Care Record Exemplars (LHCRE). The LHCRE programme was awarded to five regions with a second wave due to be launched at a later date (in 2019). The five initial exemplars were One London, Manchester, Yorkshire and Humber, Wessex, and Thames Valley and Surrey.

These exemplars were created to demonstrate and encourage the creation of regional data repositories and the sharing of information across care boundaries.

Sharing information across care settings provides the following benefits:

- Patient experience – reduces the need for patients and relatives to repeat information about the history of care at the point of care.

- Safety – having access to the entire patient record at the point of care reduces errors in due to visibility of existing conditions, treatments, allergies and medications.

- Workflow – allows workflow improvements through the sharing of information between settings, supporting earlier discharge / transfer due to requests being available to other services (such as social care).

- Avoids duplication – having access to a shared care record avoids duplicate laboratory and diagnostic testing which reduces the cost of healthcare.

- Engagement – a single accessible regional data repository allows patients to access a collective care record providing the opportunity for the patient to engage better with their care (providers) and reduces a proliferation of patient apps.

The architecture for the LHCRE programme is managed by NHS[x] and has evolved since the start of the programme. Core to the LHCRE architecture is the specification of 22 standardised national capabilities which are integral to each LHCRE, providing an underpinning foundation needed to create a national patient record network.

A broad, consolidated summary of the 22 capabilities is below:

- Security – provide an interoperable security mechanism that allows information to be securely accessed across the LHCREs (such as federated standards – OAuth/OpenID).

- Audit – ensure that all access to the information in the LHCRE platform is audited and that the audit provides a detailed level of the information accessed (who, when, what).

- Open – deliver a set of open APIs so that the information can be accessed inside and outside of the region using automated software mechanisms.

- Data Storage – a data layer that allows the storage of the data for primary and secondary use purposes. Delivery of a storage layer will enable population health as well as provide other benefits such as regional clinical decision support and real-time alerts/notification as well as pattern recognition. This capability set encompasses the need to ingest and normalise data from other sources.

- Record Location – will allow records to be found from and published to the national record location service.

- Terminology – standardises the terminologies used within the platform to agreed regional and national standards.

- Portal / User Interface – delivers a user interface that can be accessed (securely) for direct care, research and analytics.

The LHCRE programme is incredibly ambitious, especially considering the £7.5m allocated to each region. This funding provides enough for each region to procure, begin the implementation and then seek further regional ICS funding so that the platforms are sustainable.

Chapter Eighteen – GP Systems of Choice (GPSoC) and GP IT Futures

As covered previously General Practice (GP, otherwise known as primary care) is usually the first point of call for any symptoms or illness. The GP is where you go when you have any concerns with your healthcare and is where the coordination of your care should be managed. This chapter covers how GP IT is managed within the NHS and outlines the future digitalisation expectations of primary care, with an anticipated progression away from non-specialist secondary care services to an enhanced primary care model with more treatment possibilities provided in the community.

Although NHS Digital has devolved the national secondary care digital delivery strategy, NHS Digital still has control over Primary Care through the GP IT Futures procurement framework (which replaces the previous GPSoC framework). The GP IT Futures procurement framework defines the specification, standards and terms for GP IT systems and services (schedules). This means NHS Digital has contractual control over the performance, roadmap and features provided by GP system suppliers.

On the 31st January 2019 NHS England, in collaboration with the British Medical Association (BMA) published 'A five-year framework for GP contract reform to implement the Long-Term Plan'[42]. This document paves the way for GP reform, supporting General Practice as the 'bedrock' of the NHS. The document provides the framework for the needed investment in General Practice as well as the strategy to overcome staffing numbers. The document introduces the expectations for a more

[42] https://www.england.nhs.uk/wp-content/uploads/2019/01/gp-contract-2019.pdf

collaborative governance arrangement between NHS England and primary care.

In summary the framework will:

- **Resolve workload and workforce issues** – by investing £891 million of new funding in staffing by 2023/24 with a further GP core contract growth of £978 million in the same timeframe.

- **Resolve indemnity costs** – a centrally funded *Clinical Negligence Scheme for General Practice* will cover all general practice and membership to this service will be free of charge.

- **Improve the Quality and Outcomes Framework (QOF)** – by reducing the previous QOF measures and introducing a new collaborative 'test bed' approach to general practice quality measurement.

- **Automatic entitlement to Primary Care Network (PCN) contracts** – Primary Care Networks are integral to the success of the Long-Term Plan and provide the framework for GPs and other community services to come together to resolve existing resistances. Each PCN must have an accountable Clinical Director and an associated *Partnership Agreeement.*

- **Join up urgent-care services with primary care** – through the provision of direct booking agreements with the 111 service and via amendments to the extended hours contracts (the Directed Enhanced Services contract, DES). GP access and waiting times will be published monthly from 2021.

- **Digital access to primary care** – GP IT infrastructure will continue to be funded nationally with further funding available to support digital first primary care by April 2021. The framework proposes a right for patients to have preference for a digital first appointment (web and audio). Full patient record access will be available by 2020, GPs will no longer be able to advertise private GP services that are provided by the NHS. A further £20million will be made available to support the pressures of subject access requests (requests for records) on primary care.

- **Delivers more primary care services** – to support the delivery of the Long-Term Plan, the framework proposes the introduction of seven new GP services. Five of the seven start by April 2020: structured medication reviews, enhanced health in care homes, anticipatory care (with community services), personalised care and supporting early cancer diagnosis. The other two start by 2021: cardio-vascular disease case-finding and locally agreed action to tackle inequalities. All new investment will be measured through a dashboarding programme with a review on impact to ED attendances, discharges, outpatient appointments and prescribing. It is expected that this will be managed in collaboration with the Integration Care System in each region.

- **Provides funding clarity for General Practice** – £978 million is being provided to general practice through core contract adjustments by 2023/24. A new transparency framework will be introduced with GPs who earn above £150,000 a year being published by 2021.

- **Contract changes will be tested prior to introduction** – a new *test bed* programme will be introduced which allows PCNs to test any QOF, Quality Improvement or service specification change prior to introduction.

GP IT Futures is a new IT purchasing framework for primary care. The GP IT Futures programme continues to support the provision of the core IT systems for General Practice but introduces new expectations on system suppliers. Core to the modified requirements on the GP IT Futures framework is the need for IT systems to talk to each other (be open), be secure by design and use cloud native technologies. The framework introduces access to e-Consultation services, social prescribing services and other digital tools needed to deliver 21st century healthcare. A digital buying catalogue has been introduced which provides more flexibility for GP digital purchasing and there is an expectation that GP services will integrate with the NHS App – providing other service providers and patients with access to GP data.

At the time of writing 69 suppliers have been given an intention to award notification on the new GP IT Futures framework. Existing solutions are available to purchase on the 1st January 2020 (16 existing GPSoC solutions) with new solutions being evaluated against the new framework requirements over the following year.

NHS Digital funds GP IT licensing and the ongoing support and maintenance is funded through the Clinical Commissioning Group (CCG). This model holds each GP practice to account for the delivery of national digital targets. These targets have included the delivery of standardised SNOMED coding, patient access to GP records (patient access), and integration with national SPINE systems such as the Electronic Prescription Service (EPS). Further digitalisation is expected as outlined in the GP Framework above, with all GP consultations being offered digitally by 2021.

GPSoC Maturity Model

Established in 2008 and expired in December 2018, GPSoC was a 10-year contracting framework that enabled GPs to select one of four IT systems (TPP SystemOne, EMIS Web, Cegedim Vision and Microtest Evolution). Each of these systems has to comply with NHS Digital contracting requirements to retain their place on the GPSoC framework. These systems are the main providers of GP technology.

The initial GPSoC maturity model is below. This model held the suppliers and GPs to account on the delivery of strategic targets for digitalisation. It is because of this maturity model and the GPSoC framework that the NHS has one of the most digitally mature Primary Care healthcare systems in the world.

A summary of each of these maturity levels is found below:

- **Level 0** – RFA 99 (The Approved Data Model), Quality Management and System (QMAS) and Information Governance (IG). QMAS was replaced by the Calculating Quality and Reporting Service.

- **Level 1** – Level 0 plus e-Referral Service, Personal Demographic Service (PDS) access/update capability.
- **Level 2** – Level 1 plus Electronic Transmission of Prescriptions (ETP).
- **Level 3** – Level 2 plus GP records transfer capability (GP2GP).
- **Level 4** – Level 3 plus system provided as a data centre hosted solution to NHS CFH standards.
- **Level 5** – Level 4, plus access/update capability to the summary patient record held within the Personal Spine Information Service (PSIS) on the NHS CRS Spine.
- **Level 6** – Level 5, plus fully integrated with the LSP Care Record.

Close scrutiny of the model will reveal that Level 5 and 6 were never achievable due to changes in the national strategy and priorities. It also fails to include patient access in the maturity model and this is now a primary strategy for NHS Digital and a fundamental component of the NHS paperless 2020 strategy[43].

Supplier maturity was monitored and measured by NHS Digital and a supplier could only obtain accreditation at each maturity level following NHS Digital review. This approach enforced a centralised strategic delivery model and promoted an appropriate level of competitiveness in the supplier base.

GPSoC was a huge success and is one of the reasons why patients are now able to access their GP records online. It is no surprise that for these reasons the expectation is that NHS Digital may create a similar contractual framework model for secondary care.

---

[43] https://digital.nhs.uk/article/549/National-Information-Board-Paperless-2020

Chapter Nineteen – Integrated Care Systems, Sustainability and Transformation Partnerships (STPs) and Local Digital Roadmaps (LDRs)

Integrated Care Systems are an evolution of the original 44 Sustainability and Transformation Partnerships (STPs) which were created across England between healthcare organisations and local authorities. The original aim of STPs was to drive an average 2% efficiency saving and transform the way care is delivered to local populations.

This is achieved by reducing pressures on areas such as emergency care, promoting preventative care models and allowing care to be more accessible outside of the traditional care environments (hospitals and GPs). In the future, the expectation is that more care will be delivered at home and through community healthcare hubs.

Following the original plans to create STPs these areas have now progressed towards establishing Integrated Care Systems with 29 ICSs now in existence across England[44]. These "systems" bring together services by allowing[45]:

- Stronger partnerships in local places between the NHS, local government and others with a more central role for primary care in providing joined-up care.

---

[44] https://www.england.nhs.uk/integratedcare/integrated-care-systems/

[45] https://www.england.nhs.uk/wp-content/uploads/2020/11/261120-item-5-integrating-care-next-steps-for-integrated-care-systems.pdf

- Provider organisations to step forward in formal collaborative arrangements that allow them to operate at scale.

- Developing strategic commissioning through systems with a focus on population health outcomes.

- The use of digital and data to drive system working, connect health and care providers, improve outcomes and put the citizen at the heart of their own care.

Due to the fact that social care is currently managed within the Local Authority, an ICS is only a collaboration construct. This may change in April 2022 with a proposed legislative change which will transform the accountability of Integrated Care Systems. It is important to recognise that the structure of the NHS is changing and that ICSs are seen as the future commissioning, financial management and delivery vehicle for NHS services.

In the 2020 ICS next steps for integrated care publication, digital must be at the heart of each ICS[46]. The publication outlines the need for each ICS to have a board level digital SRO and the requirement for a published digital transformation plan. Each ICS must implement a shared care record, provide tools to enable collaborative working and implement published national standards. A data platform should be created and supported by a cross system analytics function to allow a complete review of pathways so that services can become digital where possible and that waste is removed from the system.

---

[46] https://www.england.nhs.uk/wp-content/uploads/2020/11/261120-item-5-integrating-care-next-steps-for-integrated-care-systems.pdf

Another aim of the ICSs/STP structures is to support the delivery of the NHS Five Year Forward View (FYFV) and Long-Term Plan. The FYFV strategy was published in 2014 with a 'next steps' update released in March 2017. These documents were further supplemented with the Long-Term Plan which was published in January 2019.

The Long-Term Plan (LTP) recognises the need to change the NHS due to capacity and affordability challenges. Within the LTP there is recognition of the need to tackle obesity, smoking and the use of drugs and alcohol. Improved education and a reduction of abuse in these areas will alleviate some of the pressure on the health service. That being said, improved public health will only alleviate the tide so the provision of healthcare needs to be balanced against the diverse population of England.

Therefore, the NHS FYFV suggested the adoption of new care delivery models such as:

- Multispecialty Care Providers, Namely Primary Care Networks (PCNs) – an example of a Multispecialty care provider would see the aggregation of services between GP's, community care, social care and mental health services to create a logical care providing service with seamless processes and patient experience across the provider network.

- Primary and Acute Care Systems (Accountable Care Systems or Integrated Care Systems) – the combining of primary care (GPs), secondary care (Hospitals) and other care services into an accountable/integrated care organisation.

- District General Hospital (DGH) sustainability partnerships – in areas where smaller and less sustainable hospitals exist, these hospitals should look to partner with larger specialist hospitals to improve care delivery, enabling economies of scale and improving care pathways where possible.

These new care delivery models are covered in the Dalton Review[47], a document that outlines new options for providers of NHS care, with more detail regarding ICS structures found in the Integrated Care Next Steps document published in November 2020[48]. All of these structures will be managed by a new Systems Oversight Framework.

Each ICS/STP strategy differs depending on the demographic. For example, some ICS/STPs are focusing on enhancing healthcare education in early year settings. A focus on health education at such a young age will reduce the pressure on our healthcare system as our children get older, increasing the productivity of the population.

There are many common themes throughout the majority of the ICS/STPs. These are:

- Improved Public Health, Prevention and Holistic Care – increase the use of analytics, education and communication to target care to those who need it most, reducing admissions and improving the overall health and well-being of the local population.

- New Care Models and Systems – it has been widely recognised that the current models of care are unsustainable and that new models and organisation

---

47

https://www.gov.uk/government/uploads/system/uploads/attachment_data/file/384126/Dalton_Review.pdf

48 https://www.england.nhs.uk/wp-content/uploads/2020/11/261120-item-5-integrating-care-next-steps-for-integrated-care-systems.pdf

structures must be developed to allow the NHS to deliver sustainable care for the future.

- Improved and Standardised Care – even though the NHS is effective at treating and managing conditions, it is likely that the same diagnosis will be treated differently depending on the organisation visited. This may result in more expensive and unnecessary care being provided in some organisations. Standardised care pathways will reduce these variations, improve patient experience and reduce the cost of care.

- Reduce the pressure on Emergency Departments – it has been well documented that A&E departments are under increasing pressure to meet the four-hour waiting target. There are many reasons for A&E waiting time delays but a large majority are due to capacity and a lack of convenient access to care services elsewhere. Improved out of hours and readily accessible access to non-emergency care, for example, the introduction of care hubs, will reduce the pressure on emergency departments.

- Train and recruit more staff into the care sector – although we are becoming healthier and living longer as a population there is still as large forecasted vacancy gap in clinical communities such as nursing, GP and acute care clinicians. This will not be helped by Brexit. There needs to be a reduction in this forecasted vacancy gap if the health service wishes to continue to deliver the same quality of care in the future.

- Enhance services out of the hospital – almost all ICS/STPs plan to reduce the amount of specialist, non-complex care delivered within hospitals. Where possible, services will be provided in the community or at home, improving the capacity issues that exist within the health service today.

- Changing the way services are commissioned – at this stage, commissioning is untenable with services costing more than the budgets available to deliver care. New group models of care will be established to develop outcome-based care models, with ICS's being held accountable for budgetary expenditure. A renewed focus on the improvement of care from both a prevention and outcome perspective is integral to future planning.

- Providing Equality to Mental Health Services – mental health is as important as physical health and therefore the development of access to mental health services must improve to ensure patients have a complete, coherent and holistic care pathway.

- Cancer and End-of-Life-Care – One in two people in the UK will obtain a cancer diagnosis at some point in their lives. Although cancer survival rates continue to improve it is important that access to quality cancer care is available to the entire population and that cancer targets continue to be a priority to the NHS. End-of-life is equally important and partnerships between hospices and end-of-life charities should be integrated into care models to support end of life care pathways.

- Supporting Long Term Conditions – almost all ICS/STPs will have a focus on changing the way long-term conditions are managed, moving from a hospital model to a community model or enabling patients to monitor conditions from home.

Following the creation of the STPs, NHS England requested the submission of Local Digital Roadmaps (LDR). These roadmaps were created to ensure that each STPs digital strategy was aligned to the national priorities as well as ensuring value for money across each demographic region. Although each LDR is diverse, each one was set the objective to ensure the following digital elements were on the agenda:

- Supporting the STP delivery – each LDR should be aligned to the local STP needs, introducing system wide analytics, patient access to records and integrated care platforms.

- Channel shift in care delivery – the LDR should introduce new channels of care such as video based consultations, tele-consultations and remote monitoring.

- Enforced use of the electronic referral service (ERS) – it is now mandatory for all initial primary to secondary care referrals to be handled using the electronic referral service.

- Provision of Wi-Fi in primary care – access to the internet should be available at all primary care sites in England.

- Delivery of the HSCN network – it is the STP and the associated digital lead's responsibility to ensure that organisations within the STP migrate to the new Health and Social Care Network.

- Improved digital transfers of care – the STP should improve the adoption of standards that allow patient information to be transferred between care-providing organisations. Transfer of care will initially focus on the transfer of discharge information between primary and secondary care using the MESH infrastructure.

- Patient access to primary care records – patients should be given access to their GP record in primary care. Access will initially include diagnosis, appointment and prescription information but will evolve into full access to the patient record in primary care.

Common to the LDRs is the support of STP priorities such as access to population analytics, enhanced primary and secondary care systems, patient access to records, improved information sharing and the development of digital infrastructure to support the STP.

Chapter Twenty – Allied Health Professionals

This book has provided insight into digitalisation in primary and secondary care. General practitioners, doctors, surgeons and nurses require an Electronic Health Record (EHR) to triage, diagnose, treat and monitor the success of patient care.

There is however another large group of care providing specialists which are also harnessing the power of digital. These are known as Allied Health Professionals (AHPs) and they range from therapists (physio, speech, occupational) to lesser-known services such as art and music therapy. There are 14 AHPs listed on the NHS England website[49] and all play a pivotal role in the diagnosis and treatment of patients.

In April 2019 a digital framework for AHPs was published by NHS England[50]. The framework focuses on three ambitions to progress the digitalisation of AHP services and aligns the AHP digital workforce with the Chief Clinical Information Officer and the Chief Nursing Information Officer as well as other senior digital officials in the NHS.

The three ambitions that the AHP digital framework proposes are:

- Ambition 1: Digital Ready AHP Services – focuses on leadership, the development of the workforce and the creation of roles that support AHPs progressing into digital careers.

---

[49] https://www.england.nhs.uk/ahp/role/
[50] https://www.england.nhs.uk/wp-content/uploads/2019/04/a-digital-framework-for-allied-health-professionals.pdf

- Ambition 2: Digitally Mature AHP Services – provides a set of expectations for the use of digital for AHP services. These are the use of electronic systems to capture notes and observations, the use of electronic prescribing to enforce safety, delivery of remote AHP solutions and using interoperability to support the transfer of care between settings.

- Ambition 3: Data enabled AHP services – progressing the use of data in AHP services to detect, prevent and reduce the variation of healthcare. The use of data by AHPs can also be used to prevent harm, provide decision support and inform alerts and notifications. Data is integral to obtaining feedback from patients and staff on their digital experiences in order to improve care.

It is clear from the framework that there is a vibrant AHP community with strong digital leadership and engagement. The framework provides clarity and understanding that digitalisation is important for the future of AHP services. The framework recognises that AHPs cannot achieve pervasive digitalisation on their own and that they are an integral part of the care continuum.

The broader 2017 AHPs into action strategy[51] highlights digital as an integral component of the future of AHP services. It should be noted that interoperability is likely to be a key requirement for AHP technology as remote therapeutic requirements are often not met by the integrated EHR vendors.

---

[51] https://www.england.nhs.uk/ahp/ahps-into-action/

Chapter Twenty-One – Artificial Intelligence

Artificial Intelligence (AI) is intelligence demonstrated by machines, and in most cases is the development of a machine/robot or piece of software/algorithm to reach a defined goal (usually replacing a function conducted by a human). AI is of importance to healthcare as it reduces the demand burden by providing additional machine-led diagnostic, analytical, or operational capacity through the identification of anomalies which then enable care providers to prioritise workloads.

AI can be used for many purposes but is most commonly used to analyse images, language or patterns in order to learn the difference between good and bad, right and wrong or translate a given phrase to an alternative language (or medical language). Although AI is extremely promising there is still a lot of work to do in the AI field as there is a need to train the machine in order to improve accuracy so that they can be used with acceptable confidence at the point of care.

Developing AI is usually conducted by the creation of AI models. These models contain the rules and methods that are used by the machine or computer to provide the result. Most AI models use probability to determine how confident the machine is that the output matches the required result. This means that AI is not 100% correct 100% of the time.

NHS[x] are supporting the development of AI in the NHS through the development of the AI Lab[52]. The AI Lab aims to support the NHS and the healthcare market to develop data-driven AI solutions that use the following AI techniques:

---

[52] https://www.nhsx.nhs.uk/ai-lab/

- Inductive logic programming – is an approach to AI where logic programming is used to prove hypothesis. This is developed by using both positive and negative inputs to train and develop the logic model to get to a probabilistic result. A set of data is then fed into the model with the most probable results returned by the model (by highest to lowest score).

- Robotic process automation (RPA) – these tools provide the ability to automate business processes by teaching a machine to carry out the same computer tasks as a human. It is often common to find these tools interacting with legacy systems which do not provide any automated form of integration (API or database). RPA removes this issue through watching a user carrying out these activities and then repeating the activities without human support (training the software to mirror the human macro).

- Natural language processing (NLP) – is the ability for the machine to read and translate written or spoken language. NLP is useful in healthcare as it can speed up the coding process by reading through the notes and inferring diagnostics, procedures or presenting complaints. NLP can also reduce the need for medical translators as machines can support clinicians to communicate with patients.

- Computer vision – this field of AI is focused on training computers to 'see' and understand images and video. Computer vision is a complex and diverse field with researchers teaching machines to identify objects, make decisions, restore images, detecting events and other disciplines. This field is arguably the most relevant to healthcare because of the development of digital pathology and machine-based diagnostics (radiology).

- Neural networks – are modelled on the human brain and are based on weighting decisions through connections between the inputs and outputs at each stage of the decision-making process. An example of a neural network is known as a 'linear regression' which can use time series data to predict the future. An issue with neural networks is that they often require vast amounts of training data in order to learn the correlation between inputs and the desired output to increase accuracy.

- Distributed artificial intelligence – may use the above methods or other concepts to distribute the machine analysis over many computer 'nodes' in a distributed network. This approach to AI is often adopted when attempting to analyse or apply models to large datasets across many organisations.

  An example of this would be the analysis of radiology images across many organisations which would be difficult to bring together, therefore a set of distributed AI agents would be deployed across the organisations with the results then fed centrally to determine the outcome.

As the more complex 'reasoning' AI is probabilistic it will take some time to become mainstream in healthcare. Machines do not yet have "commonsense reasoning" which is the ability to take a view outside of the given structured algorithms. These kinds of optimisations require human level judgements which can often result in mis-classification of results by a machine which then requires further training and optimisation in order to remove the error from the algorithm over several training iterations.

NHS[x] will play a key role in scaling and supporting the development of AI in the NHS. The team have already published a "how to get it right"[53] report alongside publishing a code of conduct. NHS[x] want to ensure that AI will scale, is being effectively governed and managed and that barriers for entry are lowered to deliver the best possible outcome for the service.

The adoption of AI in healthcare is controlled by the EU Medical Devices Regulations which may change following the UK exit from the European Union. More information can be found here: https://bit.ly/2L14szU.

---

53 https://bit.ly/2JqOnTs

Chapter Twenty-Two – The Future of Health Digitalisation

You are now coming to the end of this book and by now you should have a fair grasp on the fundamentals of Healthcare IT. A fair amount of this book covers the current state of Healthcare in the NHS with an insight into future possibilities. This chapter goes beyond these predictions and expresses the opportunities for the future of Digital Healthcare.

This book has expressed the need for prevention rather than reaction and to move to an event-driven healthcare system. An event-driven model is established by enabling patients to consistently monitor their own health and use technology to provide them with the information needed to make informed healthcare decisions.

An example of this is diabetes patients. There are an estimated four million people in the UK living with diabetes, representing 6% of the population. Some of these people are undiagnosed. The treatment of diabetes today is generally managed through continuous outpatient follow-ups over a prolonged period of time. Continually treating this volume of patients requires a significant amount of clinical and operational man-power. This approach is not cost effective for the NHS and can be resolved using technology.

Technology can assist and change diabetes care. This is possible because of the advent of home electronic diabetes monitoring devices. These devices are used by the patient at home to monitor insulin levels and there is no reason why this information cannot be fed to a centrally managed diabetes monitoring centre enabling clinicians to respond to adverse trends or alarms coming directly from the diabetes patient cohort.

Taking this scenario further, imagine a time where every person in the country could be real-time DNA[54] tested for illness or disease, providing current and predicting future conditions. Now, imagine if these tests were totally accurate, integrated with automated diagnostic monitoring, drug prescription services and linked to a centralised care command centre. This kind of model could enable just-in-time delivery of care to individuals who need it most. This kind of innovation may change the healthcare system entirely, enabling healthcare to scale with the growing change in the population.

This is somewhat possible today through services such as 23 and me[55], a service which provides DNA testing over the internet, mapping the genome to 150 traits. The cost of this service is currently £149 per test and is unaffordable for widespread NHS adoption. The cost of these tests will reduce overtime and, once mainstream, will enable patients to self-monitor at home, predicting and reporting on their current and possible future health conditions.

Another value to DNA based medicine is that drugs and treatments can be personalised to a person's genetic configuration. Using a personalised approach will reduce the cost of care as patients will receive drugs that specifically target their condition(s) and the related DNA variances that have caused the illness or disease to materialise in the first place. We may also reach a time where all genetic illnesses can be eradicated from the embryo prior to conception[56]. If disease could be eradicated

---

[54] DNA (Deoxyribonucleic acid) is molecule that forms the configuration of the human body and relays all instructions that cause change to our configuration, some of which cause illness and disease.

[55] https://www.23andme.com/en-gb/

[56] http://www.itv.com/news/2017-08-02/human-embryo-editing-breakthrough-could-eradicate-thousands-of-inherited-diseases/

prior to birth this would reduce the cost of care in the future but may introduce other challenges such as population control.

There are many ethical questions and debates to be resolved over these innovations in care. This is mainly because DNA testing is ahead of the treatment curve and just because DNA suggests you could develop a disease does not mean that you will eventually obtain the illness. A fair amount of disease develops itself through a combination of DNA (re)configuration and the environmental factors that cause the genetic changes to occur.

The sentiment above is somewhat distant from becoming a reality and in reality, we are highly unlikely to see it realised in the next 10 years. Until personalised medicine becomes a reality, the focus will remain on existing disruptive technology. A fair portion of which is still not used in the mainstream and will gain momentum in the next 5-10 years.

- Interoperability – enables digital solutions across organisations and services to interact, and supports joined up information sharing and workflow. As interoperability continues to mature, we will see the dissolving of healthcare boundaries.

  Interoperability will enable new models of care to be established as care pathways can bridge different care disciplines or services without the transcription of data and information, enabling tasks, activities and plans to be jointly owned and maintained across disciplines.

- Population Health (Analytics) – is the concept of managing healthcare on a population basis. Population Health (Analytics) brings information from the population into an analytical repository to spot patterns and trends (such as medical conditions or treatment outcome success rates). There is huge potential when information is brought together at scale as the information can also be used to spot outbreaks, manage discrete patient events or manage healthcare resources (care-professionals, drug administration, service provision) more effectively.

- Block chain – a secure, distributed, decentralised IT system that does not have a central governance or data storage point and the data network is responsible for the integrity of the data held within the network. The power of block chain is that (patient) records can be stored in the network and can only be added by an authorised party with access to the network.

  Once written to the network the data transaction cannot be changed, or deleted as this would invalidate the network. This concept has the potential to change the way health records are stored and managed, enforcing pure legitimacy of record access (audit) and the integrity of the (patient) record as the transaction registers cannot be changed once written to the data network.

- Quantum Computing – moves current computing away from silicon to atom-based instruction processing. Moving to atom-based processing provides us with the possibility to increase processing power by millions of calculations. This increase in processing power can advance the use of existing information such as DNA/genomic data, allowing the possibility to process the human genome in real time, proposing personalised treatment plans and therapies. Quantum computing will improve the performance of AI and Machine learning, enabling machines to diagnose patients and assure patient treatment.

- (Implantable) Devices, Wearables and Tricorders (Internet of Things) – the healthcare device market has the real potential to improve diagnostics and monitoring. Healthcare devices are already used routinely in disciplines such as cardiology with pace-makers used daily to save lives. This type of usage is continuing into services such as pain management with spinal cord implants.

Devices continue to evolve, becoming digitally integrated, and with this evolution we can expect to see wireless patient monitoring devices being regularly used inside and outside of the hospital environment. This kind of innovation will enable staff within the hospital to be more efficient and improve the quality of care provided to patients.

As well as diagnostic devices, technology such as intelligent or micro pills will allow diagnostics to be carried out on patients by swallowing a tiny device. These pills have limitations due to size and safety constraints but the expectation is that these could be used in the future to prevent the need for investigations that require a camera scope to be inserted into the human body.

- Self-Driving Cars and Drones – have the potential to improve patient and organ transport. Due to social or clinical reasons, some patients require private ambulances (transport) to be discharged from hospital. Self-driving care-vehicles will limit the number of staff required to transfer or discharge a patient from hospital.

  Drones also have huge potential to transport patient organs in a timely fashion and are especially important for live donor swap programmes. In this example and in the case of kidney patients, the donated organ is transported from the recipient donor partner to the recipient donor and vice-versa. These organs are often transported by motorbike but drones could replace them at some point in the future.

- Robotics – Robots have been in use in the health service for some time. Robotic pharmaceutical dispensing and robotic IT backup tape libraries have reduced the need for human intervention for over a decade. As robots become more intelligent, we could see scenarios with robot porters, robot food waiters and possibly robotic phlebotomy rounds.

  Robots are also supporting clinical operations by enabling clinicians to perform micro precision duties through the use of robotic arms and magnification workstations. The benefit of these robots is smaller incisions, improved recovery and reduced operating time.

  Looking further ahead robots could become responsible for caring for specific patient groups in the home, providing a level of emotional support, diagnostic monitoring and prescribing activities. Trained healthcare robots will also be able to deliver care to remote parts of the world where receiving healthcare is difficult.

- Virtual Reality (VR) and Augmented Reality (AR) – technology that overlays three dimensional (3D) environments in the real-world or visualise 3D models using a headset. This approach can benefit patients with mental illness or be used to retrain the brain when parts of the body fail. The use of VR and AR has been applied in mental health to assist people overcome conditions such as Obsessive Compulsive Disorder (OCD), through simulating environments that retrain people to tolerate specific situations.

VR and AR can also assist with training and staff development by enabling clinicians and staff to operate or simulate operating procedures or critical scenarios. This approach to training can accelerate accreditation processes as clinical staff can practice in simulated environments without the need to be in the operating room. Specific patient groups could also receive virtual training to help manage their particular conditions.

- 3D printing of everything – 3D printing, or more broadly known as additive manufacturing, enables us to use processes and specialist equipment to create composite objects. The benefit of 3D printing is that the manufacturing process can happen instantly using specialist local equipment.

  Additive manufacturing can be used to print personalised medication, biology (such as organs and cells), prosthetic limbs and more commonly, customised casts and moulds.

- Genomics, Optogenetics and Stem Cell Research – Genomics put very simply is the process of capturing and understanding the complete configuration of the human body. Capturing and understanding the configuration of the body allows the analysis of variances for specific disease types. This analysis enables the creation and testing of medicines that can possibly counteract or prevent these variances with the outcome of improved quality of life or life expectancy for specific patient groups.

  Optogenetics is a biological technique that uses light to control human cells. Optogenetics usually targets the function of the brain, changing specific brain behaviours. Controlling and visualising the brain's reaction using Optogenetics has many benefits for specific patient groups such as those suffering pain management, sleep disorders, Parkinson's disease and psychiatric patients.

Stem cells are able to regenerate even after a prolonged period of inactivity. Cells are one of the smallest micro components that form the human body. Stem cells have significant relevance due to their regenerative nature and that they are one of the earliest form of cell produced when humans reproduce. These early Stem cells can be manipulated to prevent disease. Research into Stem cells may enable scientists to understand how human cells regenerate and improve the body's performance to repair any kind of injury or disease.

On analysing the list above it is clear that the future of healthcare is highly dependent on digital. The list above is not exhaustive and other technologies will have an impact as digital healthcare progresses. One thing that is for certain is all clinical and non-clinical innovation will have some form of technology requirement in the future.

Chapter Twenty-Three – COVID-19

A book about health digitalisation cannot be complete without mentioning the COVID-19 pandemic. COVID-19 has single handily waved a digital magic wand over the NHS, reducing potentially years of bureaucracy to allow information sharing, rapid solution purchasing and digital implementation.

Organisations and services have worked tirelessly to deliver additional capacity (new ICU services) as well as scale digital solutions to meet demand and support the training needs of staff. NHS Digital supported this journey with the delivery of Microsoft Teams which is now at the forefront of NHS collaboration as well as a rapid delivery of Attend Anywhere, a virtual outpatient capability. NHS Digital have also delivered several COVID tracking services during the pandemic.

It is often forgotten that in the modern day almost everything is or requires digital input. ICU systems connect to ventilators and observation monitors which are plumbed into real-time central monitoring systems. Telephone systems are powered by computer networks and we simply cannot work without the EHR systems that support the day to day needs of health and social care.

COVID-19 has been seen as a bureaucracy buster[57], partly due to increased funding and overnight procurement / data sharing relaxation. Organisations have been able to use this opportunity to leverage digital in ways that were not previously common-place.

---

[57] https://www.gov.uk/government/consultations/reducing-bureaucracy-in-the-health-and-social-care-system-call-for-evidence/outcome/busting-bureaucracy-empowering-frontline-staff-by-reducing-excess-bureaucracy-in-the-health-and-care-system-in-england

Examples of digitalisation due to COVID-19 are:

- Digitalisation of patient interactions – primary and secondary care (including focus groups and therapies) have now all moved to virtual with only required services being offered face to face.

- Inpatient visitation – is now possible using bedside and/or telehealth services (such as a touch away). This provides relatives with the ability to visit loved ones without risking infection or breaching lock-down restrictions.

- Information sharing – information governance rules were relaxed to allow access to data across care boundaries, promoting faster discharge and increased collaboration between care settings.

- Agile delivery – hospitals and services have had to deliver additional capacity in areas such as ICU which has resulted in 'cookie-cutter' approaches to the expansion of services.

  IT solutions have been developed in an accelerated manner. New systems are needed to track COVID vaccinations, workforce and community testing and deliver SMS COVID test results. Additional knowledge sharing systems have been created to allow expertise to be load balanced in areas of pressure (real-time, point of care training).

- Improved staff capability – staff which were previously resistant to digitalisation are now adopting digital technology.

These are the digital benefits of such a torrid time. It remains to be seen if the level of flexibility will remain following the pandemic but for now this new approach to digital delivery is a breath of fresh air, and is seen as an opportunity to fundamentally change the approach to digitalisation in the NHS.

Closing Comments

You've now come to the end of this book; I hope you've found the content useful. As you will have gathered, there is a lot of change required in the NHS to ensure that the service is sustainable and continues to maintain its position as one of the best value healthcare systems in the world.

Technology and digital will play a vital role in the sustainability challenge. As we progress, we have the opportunity and responsibility to make a real difference to patients, carers and service-users lives. Let's try and make it enjoyable shall we.

One final comment before I close:

Adopt technology wisely, keeping the patient, carer, and care-provider at the heart of everything. Deliver valuable, transformative outcomes, not just technology, and do the utmost to provide an enjoyable digital experience that meets as many expectations as possible.

Appendix – Reading Materials

The NHS Digital Strategy
https://digital.nhs.uk/article/249/Our-Strategy

The Wachter Review
https://www.england.nhs.uk/digitaltechnology/info-revolution/wachter-review/

NIB Personalised Health and Care 2010
https://www.gov.uk/government/uploads/system/uploads/attachment_data/file/384650/NIB_Report.pdf

Dalton Review
https://www.gov.uk/government/publications/dalton-review-options-for-providers-of-nhs-care

'Confidentiality' NHS Code of Practice
https://digital.nhs.uk/article/1200/Confidentiality

Data Protection Act
https://www.gov.uk/data-protection

NHS Act 2006
http://www.legislation.gov.uk/ukpga/2006/41/contents

Optogenetics
https://www.scientificamerican.com/article/optogenetics-controlling/

Stem Cells
https://www.mayoclinic.org/tests-procedures/bone-marrow-transplant/in-depth/stem-cells/art-20048117

Analysis on AI in medical Device Legislation
https://www.cocir.org/fileadmin/Position_Papers_2020/COCIR_Analysis_on_AI_in_medical_Device_Legislation_-_Sept._2020_-_Final_2.pdf

… and Zack, Corey and Rose, with Love.

Cover Designed by Corey McAllister, Aged 10.

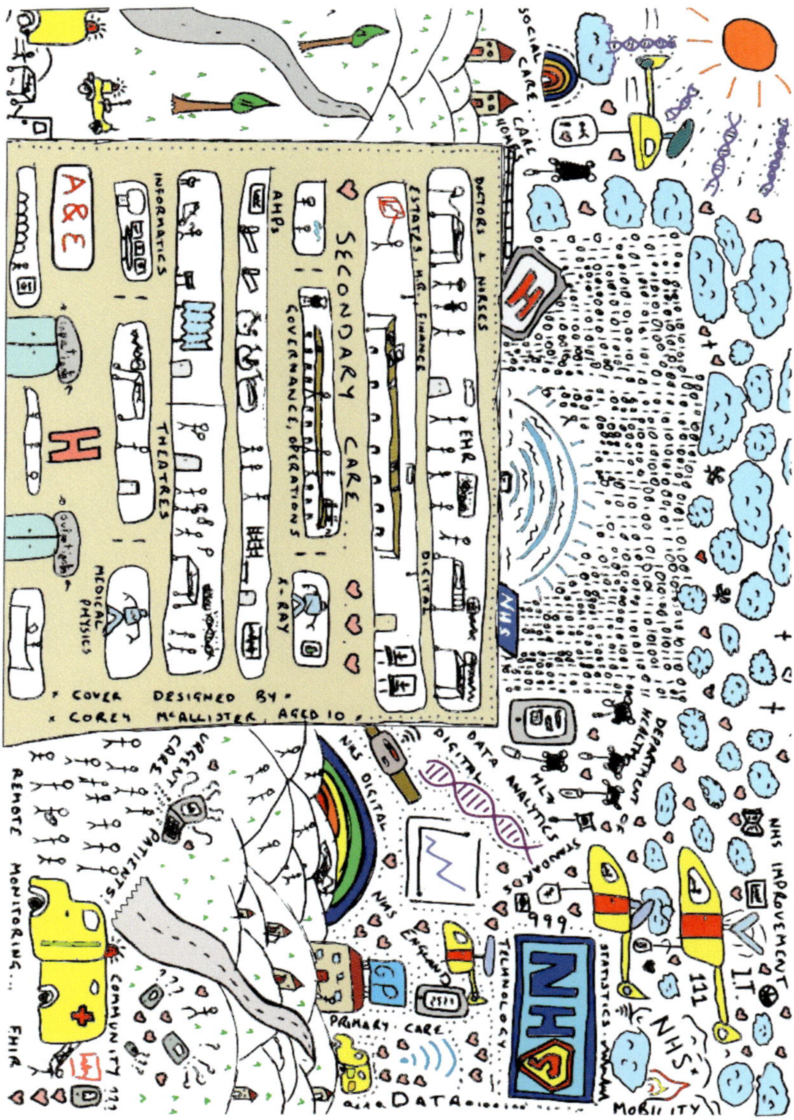

Printed in Great Britain
by Amazon

57421923R00083